Vacation Yesterdays of New England

also by William H. Marnell

The First Amendment
Man-Made Morals
Once Upon a Store: A Biography
of the World's First Supermarket
The Good Life of Western Man
The Right to Know: Media and
the Common Good

Vacation Yesterdays
of New England

William H. Marnell

A Continuum Book
THE SEABURY PRESS · NEW YORK

The Seabury Press
815 Second Avenue
New York, N. Y. 10017

Printed in the United States of America

Library of Congress Cataloging in Publication Data

Marnell, William H
  Vacation yesterdays of New England.

  (A Continuum book)
  1. New England—Social life and customs. 2. New
England—Description and travel—1865–1950. 3. Marnell,
William H.   I. Title.
F9.M34   974′.04   75-2064
ISBN 0-8164-9254-9

to
Richard and Genevieve Tyrell
and
the Crew

Contents

List of Illustrations

Vacation Yesterdays of New England

An old-fashioned summer hotel.

1. Birth of an idea

 The rarest of the gods' gifts to man is a new idea. The idea that passes as new usually is a new twist to an old idea, or a new development from an established idea. The idea that is truly new, that has no ancestry or collateral relatives, that comes into being by spontaneous generation, visits the earth less frequently than the rarest of comets, but once it has arrived, unlike the comet, it is here to stay. An idea need not be momentous to be new nor need it be momentous in its nature to be momentous in its effects. The idea that the steam escaping from the spout of a kettle might be contained, compressed and systematically released so as to do work was not momentous in its nature, although few new ideas have been more momentous in their effects. The idea of the vacation was a new idea of the steam kettle sort, not momentous in its nature but destined to create one of the major industries of the modern world and to give certain strips of sun-kissed coast and certain ridges with snow-capped peaks an economic and even a political importance they never would have had if that new idea had not been born. Florida and Switzerland are examples.

In what inspired mind the idea of vacation had its spontaneous generation no one can say. There is no evidence that it was in the mind of an employer. Since there must be some primal matter out of which the newest of ideas emerges, the best bet is that behind the idea of the vacation were two other ideas, one very ancient and one quite modern, the idea of the leisure class and the idea of retirement. The vacation connotes a sampling of the former and a preview of the latter. Whether there ever has been in the strict sense of the term a leisure class may perhaps be questioned. Most right-thinking members of the European aristocracy have worked hard at the job of being aristocrats and historically the job has called for more estate management, employee relationships and trafficking in merchandise than equalitarians have always conceded. There have always been loafers, however, and the basis for distinguishing the idle rich from the idle poor has been less a philosophy of existence than the fiscal basis which sustained or failed to sustain that philosophy. As for the capitalists of nineteenth-century America who were in a fiscal position to buttress a philosophy of idleness after the fashion of sheiks and emirs of oil-rich Araby, the truth is that they worked as though possessed by the traditional demons, and they kept on working until such then undiscovered fiends as tension and cholesterol undid them. But they had their hours of relaxation, and they relaxed with the same intensity with which they worked. The fierce relaxation of the American financial mogul, like the less self-conscious relaxation of the European aristocrat, furnished one model for the vacation.

Retirement was another. Retirement is the product of an instinct for the happy ending. One tenable thesis is that the French have given that instinct the freest play, and certainly the French have perfected the concept of retirement as thoroughly as they have perfected the concept of cooking. The French work hard and with specific goals in mind, and one of the goals is the golden years which are the interest diligence pays to the one who has deposited energy and thought in the savings account he calls his life. When the time comes, he ceases to work and he lives on his savings and this is precisely what he has intended to do all along. The wisdom of the French in this matter is now imitated with greater or less success by other peoples, sometimes as the matter of personal conviction which has been the pole star of the Gaul and sometimes as a matter of occupational policy worked out through negotiation between management and labor. One thing is certain: the philosophy behind Social Security, that one's working lifetime grinds to a gradual halt and Social Security takes up some of the fiscal slack as the end approaches, has never been really accepted and is today

in the main forgotten. Most Americans now expect to retire
and have plans to that end. The paid vacation is a foretaste
of the retirement delights.

Our subject is not the vacation as it is today. Library
shelves groan with books on that subject. There is hardly a
nation in the world that is not the vacation land of some
book or other, or for that matter hardly an American state,
and the lands that are blessed with our already mentioned
sun-kissed coasts or snow-capped peaks have become sub-sec-
tions of literature itself. Behind the books is the basic fact:
the vacation has brought into being one of the great
industries of America and Europe, and today there are states
and nations in which the leisure of persons from other parts
is the cornerstone of the economy. Once more Florida and
Switzerland are obvious examples. Our concern is the vacation of yesterday, not the momentous development but the
simple beginnings, not the Industrial Revolution, so to speak,
but the steam escaping from the kettle spout which had the
capacity of being compressed and made to do work. The
justification for recalling yesterday in this matter would not
seem difficult to establish. In some respects the yesterday of
the paid vacation is quite literally yesterday. One does not
have to be an ancient of days to recall when it was a new and
glorious idea, an idea one could hardly believe to be true. It
had that irresistible enticement that something for nothing
always has, and one felt the enticement even as one stoutly
denied that it was something for nothing. The writer recalls
his first experiences with the paid vacation. It was at a large
food store by which he was employed, a gargantuan place
which anticipated the modern supermarket in many respects
and surpassed it in others.

Management announced at the start of one summer that
the full-time help were about to get paid vacations. They
would run from Monday through Thursday on two successive
weeks. Naturally workers would be expected back on the job
Friday and Saturday when the store was really busy. It was
a primitive sort of vacation arrangement and one may
properly question if it would meet the most austere standards of the AFL-CIO, but it broke new ground where ground

had barely been prodded before. But this store had a fascinating way of being ahead not only of its own times but of these times. There was the week when the floodgates opened and it rained cats and dogs from Monday through Thursday. The following Monday a notice was posted: *Anyone who got stuck with last week off can have another week to make up for it after Labor Day.* We are not certain that even today the austere AFL-CIO standards include that sort of rain insurance.

There remains little to say by way of introduction except the caveat that no individual is ever present at the multiple accouchements of new ideas. One imagines that the vacation was a new idea at much the same time in many parts of America, but the writer's direct memory has the city of Boston as its focal point, with the rest of New England, New York, New Jersey and some rather thin salients to points farther west within its circumference. Therefore he has limited his literary researches, to dignify unworthily some very entertaining reading, to these areas. He has done so in

New York Public Library

The arrival of the mail was an important daily event at the resort hotel.

the confidence that there are some human institutions fundamentally the same wherever found, once the facade is penetrated and the inner reality reached. An old-fashioned summer hotel can be recognized at once, whether in the White Mountains of New Hampshire or the Rocky Mountains of Colorado. A camp beside a lake in Maine is indistinguishable from a camp beside a lake in Minnesota. And so, when we turn back the pages labeled Massachusetts or New York or Maine, they could be labeled quite as well South Carolina or Wisconsin or California. If the reader of any book honestly expects to get something from it, even something so pleasantly fugitive as the momentary remembrance of pleasant things past, he must bring to it the creative imagination and with it draw equations. Thus a beach in Maine equates with a beach in Mississippi; a family-sized climbing mountain in New Hampshire equates with a size ten foothill in Wyoming; a rocking-chair brigade in Vermont matches its sedentary counterpart in Indiana. As the ancients put it, *De te fabula*. We shall try to tell the story, but the story is about you. For Massachusetts or Maine, New York or New Jersey, read whatever state you may remember. Thoreau saw the whole world in Concord, and so can anyone who uses his eyes as Thoreau used his.

2. Medicine waters of the Great Spirit

 The American vacation started as a by-product of the search for health and the search for salvation. It had to start in some such fashion, because it started in the nineteenth century and that century well knew that the idle mind is the devil's workshop and the idle body is under management at least as bad. Therefore vacation without extenuating circumstances could never be anything but idleness. No one in the nineteenth century, however, would speak of the search for salvation with other than profound respect, and the search for health enjoyed then at least some of the charisma that surrounds it now. When the search for health ceased to be the undiluted preoccupation of the searcher and something extraneous, probably reprehensible, but certainly titillating, crept in, to wit, enjoyment, the vacation was born.

One may peer into the mists of antiquity and see emerging even then something like the fusion of vacation and the search for health. The Spartans may have gone to Thermopylae to save Greece from the Persians, but the Corinthians went there to loll about the hot springs. Some Romans went to Cumae to consult the Sybil, but more went to luxuriate in sun and sand. Europeans through the centuries have known that there is no more pleasant way to regain health, or to bolster up the good health you already have, than to take a room at a good hotel at one of the hot springs and for a week or two delicately balance the regimen by health-promoting activities at the spa by day and health-diminishing activities at the casino by night. No one ever doubted how the balance would point, when the week or two were over. It was "the cure" they had taken, and it was never called anything else.

The American vacation was born in New York, at a health resort called Saratoga Springs. Who first sought health at Saratoga and why he thought he could find it there is unknown. It is known that he was an Indian. In 1767 the Indians brought Sir William Johnson, British Superintendent of Indian Affairs, to Se-rach-to-que, which means by one translation "Floating scum upon the water," and by a translation more acceptable to the Saratoga Chamber of Commerce, "Hillside country of a great river." Sir William would appear to have been the first white man to visit Saratoga. He may have visited it for health, or for curiosity, but certainly not for vacation.

Cleveland Amory, in his indispensable *The Last Resorts*, quotes an 1821 guidebook on the subject of Saratoga waters and their therapeutic blessings:

The most prominent and perceptible effects of these waters when taken into the stomach are Cathartick, Diuretick, and Tonick. They are much used in a great variety of complaints; but the diseases in which they are most efficacious are, Jaundice and billious affections generally, Dyspepsia, Habitual Costiveness, Hypochondrical Complaints, Depraved appetite, Calculous and nephritic complaints, Phagedenic or ill conditioned species or states of gout, some species of dropsy, Scrofula, paralysis, Scorbutic affections and old Scorbutic ulcers, Amenorrhea, Dysmenorrhea, and Chlorosis.

More eloquent testimony to the medicinal worth of Saratoga waters can hardly be requested, nor easily elicited, and the water indeed tastes bad enough to be quite possibly good for you. This writer has not identified by personal observation at Saratoga any of the 1821 complaints catalogued, with the likely exception of "Depraved appetite," and he leaves to the totally competent Spa Association the entirely professional medical work done at Saratoga. This is not his concern. The fish he has to fry come from waters without "Cathartick," "Diuretick," or "Tonick" worth.

Leaving out the Indians, whose motivations stay inscrutable, and Sir William Johnson who probably was just curious,

New York Public Library

Congress Spring, in the public park, Saratoga Springs, New York.

the first whites to seek out Saratoga undoubtedly did so for one of the several health reasons cited in the guidebook quoted above. But the seeker for health at a spa is not a hospital patient and never was one, or at least never was one in the early nineteenth century when there were no hospitals at spas. There were hotels, and there was a hotel at Saratoga as early as 1802. Unless one's health is very bad indeed, it is hard to eliminate enjoyment entirely from a stay of a week or two at a good country hotel. But Saratoga, by the inescapable facts of geography, was no place for the desperately stricken to reach, since in the early nineteenth century it was a desperately difficult place to reach even for the robust.

The nearest city is and always has been Albany, some thirty or more miles away, then no trivial distance and not a trivial drive even in the twentieth century until the Northway was built. The Hudson is not too practical a river beyond Albany and at its nearest point it is a dozen miles or so east of the Springs. Travel from New York City meant a long boat trip up the river capped by a long stagecoach ride, and travel from Boston meant the passage of the Berkshires, a range of mammoth proportions in the early 1800s. Travel from elsewhere was simply quixotic to contemplate, so no one contemplated it. The inescapable conclusion is that those beset by "Dyspepsia, Habitual Costiveness, Hypochondrical Complaints" and similar ailments were not so gravely stricken as not to be able to enjoy a week or so in a good country hotel, and the better the waters made them feel the better they could enjoy it.

The American spa, whether it be Saratoga Springs, its predecessor the unassuming Stafford Springs in northeast Connecticut, such estimable rivals for the southern trade as Hot Springs and White Sulphur Springs, automatically provided vacations as by-products of cures. That to take the cure was also to take a vacation would go without saying in Europe, and if the vacation aspect was deficient in quality,

Those beset by dyspepsia and similar ailments were not so gravely stricken as to be prevented from enjoying a week or so in a good country hotel.

complaints would pierce the skies of Bath in England, Baden-Baden in Germany, Bad Gastein in Austria and the other European spas, but Europeans were little bothered by Puritanism and its corollaries, and this included the English who patronized Bath. In the United States, the story was different. Here Puritanism was epidemic in the North, and stirred uneasily beneath the Anglicanism of the South. The first American to take a vacation was the man taking the cure at Saratoga Springs who slowly forgot the work ethic, expanded into comfortable living, and then slipped quietly into general relaxation at a Saratoga Springs hotel while his health perceptibly improved.

At this point one must establish something fundamental about the hotel, or at least about the good resort hotel. Hotel owners, for some inscrutable reason, frequently include among the advertised charms of their establishments their "homelike atmosphere." Such a claim is as groundless and nonsensical as, to the discriminating, it would be repulsive if believed. To the credit of the innkeepers of Miami Beach and the Catskills they fall victim to no such fantasy. Can one imagine the claim of homelike atmosphere for Grossinger's or the Concord, the Fontainebleau or the Eden Roc? The actual truth is that the less the atmosphere of a hotel is homelike, the better the hotel. A person on vacation leads a life different from his daily life. Therefore, in a manner of speaking, he pretends to be someone he is not. The oldest form of the pretense, one of the most satisfying, and in the whole wide world the commonest, is the pretense that on vacation one is an aristocrat.

An aristocrat lives in a palace, is waited on by liveried servants, his every want anticipated, his every whim indulged, and above all his palate tempted and satisfied with the finest of foods and the noblest of drinks. Anyone can play at being an aristocrat in a good resort hotel. It is a splendid game and Europeans have played it since the Romans created the first real summer resort at Cumae. No Europeans have enjoyed it more than the real aristocrats, who have found it so pleasant a contrast to life in a real palace that they have always been among the best customers of luxury summer hotels. Consequently, in the specific form of the vacation known as the cure, there is a fusion of several elements: the curative powers of waters which increase in direct ratio to the repulsiveness of their taste, the comforts and the luxuries of a hostelry in which every conscientious effort is made at eliminating anything remotely suggestive of a homelike atmosphere, and the presence of a clientele adequately financed by conscientious dedication to the work ethic to afford the luxury of pretending to be aristocrats who inherited their wealth and do not work at all. Therefore the best area on which to focus if one would analyze the beginnings of the American vacation is hotel row.

New York Public Library

Broadway, Saratoga Springs, 1927, with its array of grand old establishments.

The Grand Union Hotel was in Saratoga Springs by 1836 and was there by 1864 in the expanded majesty that an older generation still remembers. The United States Hotel was there as well, and it lives in awesome memory a generation after its decease. Once more to borrow from Mr. Amory's research, the Grand Union had a dining room one hundred yards long, a solid mahogany bar, a porch that measured over a quarter of a mile, an acre of marble, twelve acres of carpeting, and a clientele that included Lillian Russell and

Diamond Jim Brady. It is clear that Saratoga was a place that may have been a health resort but was something more. That it became dedicated to the improvement of the breed of horses and also to the improvement of the breed of bettors by the experiential method, reinforces the impression that Saratoga quickly turned to other demigods than Aesculapius. To be succinct, the patron of the one-hundred-yard dining room and the solid mahogany bar, of Canfield's Club House and the Saratoga track, whether or not he took a passing draught from the Medicine Waters of the Great Spirit, was on vacation and nothing else. It might even be argued that Saratoga would do the likes of him more physical harm than good, no matter how much it refreshed his spirit and polished the ebullience with which he viewed the passing scene.

The tradition of the aristocratic vacation, we repeat, is a very ancient one, and a tradition to which historians of conspicuous expenditure might well address themselves. Roman patricians lounging at the Baths of Caracalla, Beau Nash on self-display in the gardens of Claverton Manor outside Bath, Dr. Faust taking the waters at his native Bad Kreuznach on the Nahe, town of roses and nightingales, and the crusaders bathing in the Bassin des Ladres at Ax-les-Thermes in the Pyrenees, which Louis IX built for those who returned with leprosy, are in that ancient line. The vacation of the lord blends with the vacation of the one pretending to be a lord. The pretense with intent to deceive blends with the innocent pretense with no such intent at all and no objective except the innocent enjoyment of unaccustomed luxury. All this Europe had for centuries before America had Saratoga, but Saratoga is irreplaceable and precious as one of the places that showed America how to do it.

Saratoga was the creation of our native, home-grown, American aristocracy. The feet that rested on the foot rail at Canfield's bar had earned the right to rest there by winning the way to the top in the no-holds-barred competition of nineteenth-century *laissez faire* America. The patrons of Saratoga were the aristocracy of the soil, the untouched top soil of America that had grown in richness for centuries beyond reckoning, the aristocracy of the minerals beneath it which nature had hoarded, the aristocracy of the unfelled forests, the unsullied rivers, the unopened continent and theirs was the earth and the fullness thereof because they had the enterprise, the initiative, the imagination, the energy, the indomitable will and inflexible determination— and the darker attributes deliberately barred from the list were present too—to make the earth and the fullness thereof their own. The dream was that they were noblemen, the American heirs of Edward the Black Prince and Bertrand Du Guesclin the Eagle of Brittany, in their nobility of soul and that they were heirs to the Guelphs and Ghibellines in their Homeric struggles for economic dominion. Perhaps, if we knew more about the Black Prince and the Eagle of Brittany, about the ducal houses of Brunswick and Hohenstaufen, it would turn out that they were right.

It is extremely important for a democracy to have an aristocracy of the proper sort. Man is an imitative animal and what he imitates determines in substantial measure what he is. Somewhere in every land, democratic quite as well as totalitarian, is an ideal of living embodied in some class and consequently serving as a model for those who aspire to achieve in their own lives the respected and accepted ideal. There must always be a model available for Walter Mitty. A nation is the better off for a periodic reappraisal of its model, and there is nothing America needs more today than an agonizing reappraisal of its models. By and large the model most often imitated in the western world has been the hereditary aristocrat, and when he was sufficiently motivated by *noblesse oblige* he has been about as satisfactory a model as frail human nature is apt to provide. Whether America as a whole is the better for the fact that Saratoga Springs set a pattern for the resort hotel which can be traced without a break until we reach the latest, most fabulous and not until next year to be surpassed palace for paying guests at Miami Beach is a question we hand over to the philosophers. American resort hotels, at least, have been the better for it.

The importance of Saratoga to our story increases greatly

if one understands that Saratoga for our purpose is not a place but a category, a category that includes Hot Springs, White Sulphur Springs and by a somewhat uncertain extension toward the present, Palm Springs. The eastern spas started as places where people sought health, and yet one has an uneasy feeling that the jest is tinged with truth that their waters would do no harm to those of sound health. Certainly they were not sought by those genuinely stricken by disease. If Saratoga was difficult of access, consider what access used to be to the rugged mountain fastnesses where Hot Springs and White Sulphur lurk. The "general relaxation" to be obtained at European spas was also to be obtained at their American equivalents, and general relaxation has a way of blossoming into full blown vacation. Vacation was possible at Saratoga, even in the high noon of the work ethic, because vacation was a by-product of the search for health, and being healthy has always ranked with being wealthy and wise in the adage.

Thus Saratoga provided the oldest, most fully recognized, and in the minds of many, the one true form of vacation, and it has certainly been the most abiding. It is the vacation in which one assumes the role, prerogatives and comforts of the aristocrat in his castle. The vacationer's castle is the summer hotel, and as Shaw proved statistically in *Arms and the Man* no real castle begins to have as many sheets and pillowcases as a summer hotel in Switzerland. The tycoons of the Grand Union and the United States play-acted as aristocrats in the tradition of the Black Prince and the Eagle of Brittany, and those who spent the last two in July at good, sound, comfortable, even luxurious summer hotels were aristocrats after the pattern of the tycoons of the Grand Union and the United States. The Medicine Waters of the Great Spirit may or may not have wrought physical cures, but they certainly wrought miracles of pleasant and harmless self-deception, and such is the veritable essence of vacation. Every guest is a lord in a good summer hotel.

3. *Jumping fish and salvation*

 The first analyst of the vacation psychosis was
Geoffrey Chaucer (c. 1340–1400), who, all literary critics
agree, was eminent as a psychologist. Chaucer records in the
opening lines of his *Canterbury Tales*, a work comprising the
yarns swapped on a vacation trip as yarns have been
swapped in railroad club cars and aerial cocktail lounges by
travelers in centuries after Chaucer, that the psychosis
begins to stir in April. Chaucer found an external source for
the psychosis. It coincides with April whose showers melt the
frozen earth and make the green shoots appear, April that
stirs the hearts of little birds to sing and the hearts of men
and women to seek the open road. But Chaucer was English,
a people quite as beset by the work ethic as their descendants
the Americans. Suddenly, when all is building up to a song of
the open road, the note of salvation is heard. In April,
Chaucer assures us, people long to go on pilgrimages.

This coincidence between an increase in piety and an
improvement in the weather is vital to our subject. The
improvement in the weather is a much more leisurely affair
in western New York than in southern England and the
pilgrimage to Chautauqua a much safer business in the high
noon of summer than when April is laughing her girlish
laughter all too briefly and shedding her girlish tears for
hours on end. Well over a hundred years ago farmers of
western New York longed to go on pilgrimage to Chautauqua Lake. They piled their wives and children, pots and pans
into buckboards, hitched the horses, and headed to the camp

grounds at Fair Point for a few days of swimming and salvation, the latter provided by the Methodist preachers who operated the camp meeting grounds.

The connection between the prehistory of Chautauqua and the history of the Sunday School Assembly which started on August 12, 1874, is tenuous but it exists. It is something more than the fact that Chautauqua is a fine lake and Fair Point a delightful place. The real connection is provided by the fact that people sought salvation in its rustic reaches at a time of year when rustic reaches are at their best and most attractive. That salvation has never been a twenty-four hour business is an ancient theological complaint, and reasonable theologians are content if salvation is diluted with nothing more reprehensible than swimming. There is a further point to be observed. Whatever Se-rach-to-que, alias Saratoga, meant, no philologist has ever questioned that *Chautauqua* means "jumping fish."

There is no instinct more deeply ingrained in man than the instinct to fish. Observe, then, how perfect the blend of

Fly fishing.

New York Public Library

values that Chautauqua offered to the farmers of western New York in the quiet doldrums that dirt farming can provide in mid-summer: a swim in waters that make coy advances and shy retreats along a sandy shore, a couple of hours in the boat out where the fish jump, and then the tug at the collar, the convolutions to throttle a red neck unused to the constraints of a flowing tie, all the preparations for a bout with salvation at the meeting grounds. The aspect of the work ethic with religious overtones is satisfactorily met. Salvation is pursued, but the pursuit is relieved by a swim and a mess of fish to fry. Just as it was impossible to seek health at Saratoga without having a vacation, so it was impossible to seek salvation at Chautauqua without a vacation too.

So far our dealings have been with the prehistory of Chautauqua. Its true history began, as we have said, on August 12, 1874, when the Sunday School Assembly was opened at Fair Point with forty young men and women in attendance. It came into being after this fashion. There was a wealthy manufacturer of farm machinery named Lewis Miller who lived in Akron, Ohio. There was a minister of the Methodist Episcopal Church named Reverend Dr. John Hugh Vincent. Dr. Vincent was distressed by the poor quality of the teaching done in the Sunday Schools, and believed it could be improved by a summer training institute. Dr. Vincent met Mr. Miller, convinced him of the soundness of the idea, and Mr. Miller convinced Dr. Vincent that Chautauqua Lake was the place to locate it. Dr. Vincent met the problem of poor Sunday School teaching head on by giving the remedial instruction himself. One of his teaching devices was an enormous outdoor relief map of Palestine on which he located all points of Biblical significance and could point out to his students the routes of Old Testament journeys and the sites of New Testament events. There was never anything small scale in the thinking of Dr. Vincent and Mr. Miller, and this included the outdoor relief map. On the other hand, the story that a traveling salesman in his cups once fell off Mount Sinai and was found the next morning lying face down in the Dead Sea probably is apocryphal.

A lecture in the amphitheatre, Chautauqua, New York.

The problem of the proper employment of spare time arose. Fishing from a boat, even where fish jump, is an occupation more attractive to those of sedentary and philosophic years than to young men and women. The dangers of mixed bathing, even to young people with Sunday School proclivities, are too well known to be stressed here. The forces of evil, loosely identified as wine, woman and song, had to be reckoned with. Wine, fortunately, was no problem. Chautauqua grapes are table grapes which may be manufactured into unfermented grape juice. It is not without significance that the all-time Chautauqua performer was William Jennings Bryan, who did almost as much for unfermented grape juice as Dr. Welch himself. The wine grapes came from secular regions to the east, around Keuka Lake. There were women at Chautauqua, to be sure, but Chautauqua women were to be feared for, not feared. That left song the one remaining peril, and song was rigidly excluded from Chautauqua. It was decades before secular song profaned the Chautauqua air, and then it was purified by its patriotic content.

All this, however, is negative. The problem of spare time had to be solved by positive action. Inspiration pointed to a man with a potential for unsurpassed positive action, William Rainey Harper, who later became president of the University of Chicago. As director of education at Chautauqua, Mr. Harper added secular subjects to the religious curriculum, including arts and crafts and what today would be called home economics. Chautauqua flourished, and like everything that flourishes it became diluted. Little by little the improvement of the Sunday School dwindled in importance. Little by little the unabashed seeker of culture apart from salvation came to Chautauqua to profit by the instruction offered in secular subjects. Then the inevitable happened: Chautauqua was profaned by those who came to fish and swim and were brazenly indifferent to culture and salvation alike. They were vacationists pure and simple, and Chautauqua after its fashion had gone the way of Saratoga after its very different fashion. It did not take long. Jericho may be considered fallen when U.S. Grant who drank, smoked, belonged to no church but was a friend of Dr. Vincent, appeared as a speaker. The union of Protestantism and Republicanism has always been a fruitful one; of such are silent majorities made. General Grant got the Chautauqua salute, the silent waving of handkerchiefs. You do not clap hands in church.

The history of Chautauqua would bring us into areas remote from our subject and unless the line of ancestry is borne in mind seemingly unrelated to it. For example, the Chautauqua Literary and Scientific Circle was founded and the Chautauqua Press began to roll. Out of Chautauqua came home-reading and correspondence courses and thus from the fertile seedbed of Chautauqua came the correspondence school. Chautauqua was imitated to the degree that by the turn of the century there were some two hundred chautauquas in America, housed by lakes from Maine to California and offering the best musicians, orators, masters

Viewing regattas was a popular pastime at the lakeside and the seashore

of humorous anecdote and entertainers of whatever description ingenuity could concoct and chautauquans would accept. The common denominators were a lakeside site, programs of instruction carefully tailored to the easily satisfied summer zest for learning, and paid entertainment to keep people coming for whom sylvan glades and bosky dells, and even lakes in which fish jumped, were not sufficient entertainment in themselves.

Thus another line of ancestry links Chautauqua to the summer school conducted in some rustic setting shrewdly calculated to the proper blending of intellectual enrichment with pleasurable vacation activity, such as the Breadloaf School in Vermont or the summer sessions at Aspen, Colorado. But there is a stem of the same line that blossoms with resorts at which nature's attractions are buttressed and embellished by paid entertainment of the most highly esteemed and comparably priced order. Such are to be found in the Catskills, Lake Tahoe and Las Vegas, and one says this with an awareness that there is also winter and Miami. It may be disconcerting that the Breadloaf School and Grossinger's are labeled cousins of the stock of Chautauqua, but genealogy is an exact and implacable science.

It is time to return to the farmers of precultural Chautauqua, since our concern is not the evolution of culture, intellectual or ethical, nor the ancestral line of the summer school or the correspondence course. We rule out of consideration that aspect of Fair Point which pointed toward salvation, and limit ourselves to the aspect of waters that lapped and fish that jumped. But to establish our point, we must return for a moment to Saratoga, to pick up a thread of thought only partially woven into the fabric of vacation by the Medicine Waters of the Great Spirit.

We pointed out that the person on true vacation changes his basic pattern of living. He pretends, in an entirely innocent, blameless sense of the term, to be someone he is not. He is still John Smith, husband of Mary Smith, but at Saratoga they were Sir John and Lady Smith. They lived in their crenelated castle, were served by flunkies whose livery easily outstripped Europe's noblest and rivaled that of the magnificos who served in the palaces of the cinema at its apogee, and dined very literally on the fat of the land, transferring much of its essence to their physical selves. Theirs was one of the basic vacations, the vacation of the commoner pretending to be an aristocrat.

In a fashion in some respects similar and in others profoundly different, the farmers of Fair Point pretended to be other than they really were. Barring from consideration the aspect of the visitation which concerned salvation, they wore their oldest clothes, they lived in tents, they swam in Chautauqua Lake, they fished farther out where the fish jumped, they loafed about smoking ill-flavored and worse smelling pipes and swapping yarns. Their squaws—it is futile to pretend any longer that for most of the time at Fair Point they were white men, farmers and Methodists to boot—gratefully let as much of the nineteenth century slip from their shoulders as current tolerance of dress and manners would allow, let the children run about in that approximation of wildness that the rules of the day and age, when relaxed, permitted, swapped recipes and gossip, and primal peace rested like a benediction on them for some blessed days. We no more claim primacy in the name of Chautauqua than we did in the name of Saratoga, but Chautauqua did exhibit at an early date that other pattern of vacation which is native American and well beloved. At Saratoga one pretended to be an aristocrat. At Chautauqua one pretended to be an Indian. At the heart of every American vacation is the one pretense or the other. The degree of completeness varies from person to person, place to place, time to time, but one of the two fundamental patterns emerges triumphantly through every change of person, place and time.

There is no problem to the aristocratic vacation. Its history is clear enough and its American pattern conforms well enough to that of Europe. The real problem is presented by the origins of the native American vacation, the vacation in which one puts on his old clothes, goes to a summer cottage or camp, or lives in a tent; fishes, hunts, lies around and loafs; does without the amenities of life and finds that his happiness increases as the necessities are dispensed with. That is not the European pattern of vacation, except to the extent that some aspects of European life have been Americanized. Our thesis is that this native American vacation is patterned after the white American's idea of the life of the Indian. That it is a romanticized, distorted, idealized concept makes no particular difference. It is no more so than the bourgeoisie's idea of the aristocrat's life.

Long ago the white American overpowered the Indian, and the process of the conquest fills the hearts of his descendants with shame. Whether consciously or not, the conqueror has always had a deep-rooted respect and admiration for the defeated red man. It shows itself in many ways. Towns, lakes and rivers by the hundreds bear Indian names. That is natural enough since place names are little prone to change, but local inhabitants take a certain pride in spelling out their meaning. An even greater pride is manifested in the boast of many Americans of having Indian blood. With a bland indifference to the inconsistency of their treatment of the Indian, many Americans are happy to identify with him primarily as a warrior but also as a fiercely independent individualist.

The Indian in literature is almost invariably a hero. Washington Irving contrasts the generosity and trust of the native Indian with the guilt and treachery of the white settlers in his story of King Philip's War. James Fenimore Cooper gave to American boyhood the ideal of Uncas in *The Last of the Mohicans*. Even the unfavorable portraits of the Indian, which picture him as cruel, never picture him as cowardly. Hence it is conventional for athletic teams to symbolize their prowess by adopting as their names some term identifying them with the stamina, daring and skill of the real Indians (the Braves, the Redskins, the Warriors, the Chiefs, or simply the Cleveland Indians). Small boys at the turn of the century pranced about in Indian suits, like Homer's warriors terrible with their war helmets and their brandished bows and arrows. Some of them grew up to join a fraternal order called The Noble Order of Redmen.

The use of the word *noble* is particularly significant. It has to do with the Indian's courage but there is a sense in which it refers to something else. The tenacity of the Indian in holding to a way of life of his own is regarded with awe and envy by many caught up in the turmoil of modern life and entangled in its frustrating complexities. The Indian is close to the soil, to the great spaces of the land, to its forests and its plains. He is attuned to the seasons, and he has never betrayed the world of nature. It is not without significance that parts of the United States which have become primary vacation lands are parts where the Indians still live. Northern Wisconsin and Minnesota are Indian country in both senses of the phrase, country suitable to Indian life and country where Indians live. They are also two of the prime vacation areas of America. The same is true of Arizona and New Mexico, and it would be true of northern New England if more than a tiny handful of Indians remained there. That is Indian country too.

We do not wish to be portentous about this, and even more we wish to avoid the appearance of subtle psychologizing. We do know that there is a pattern of vacation unique to this country and Canada, except to the extent that it has been imitated elsewhere, and that it is consistent with the pattern of Indian life as romantically conceived by white Americans and Canadians. American life owes far more to the Indians than is generally known or usually conceded. But the Indians of this book are not red men. They are very pale city dwellers, fugitives for the last two weeks of July from the routine of daily living commonly called civilization, intent on becoming nature's noblemen until two weeks from Monday, in the fashion that they understand and enjoy.

The two patterns of vacation merely begin to emerge at Saratoga and Chautauqua, and quite understandably each emerging pattern slips out from under the protective covering of something quite different from vacation. The farmer came to Chautauqua to seek salvation when the weather best fitted salvation outdoors, and he play-acted in the process at being an Indian. Salvation was the excuse and a vacation the by-product, just as health was the excuse at Saratoga and vacation the by-product. It is not as yet part of the record how many achieved salvation at Chautauqua, but neither is it a matter of ascertainable record how many achieved health at Saratoga. What is certain is that vacations were achieved at both places, and have been achieved yearly ever since.

The vacation aspect of life at Chautauqua was present, admitted, encouraged and organized once the Sunday School Assembly started. For that reason we find the informal Chautauqua of the New York farmers that preceded the Assembly more suited to our purpose, because it is more prophetic of the vacation pattern that Americans were to achieve spontaneously and without organization or direction. Leaving out of consideration all pseudo-romanticism that deals with the noble son of the soil, one still must recognize that the dirt farmer is in large measure his own master. He patterns his life as nature instructs him to pattern it, to be sure, but nature is seldom too demanding of the dirt farmer. There are periods when nature demands close to twenty-four hours a day attention from him, but there are also periods when nature takes over and leaves him relatively free. Dirt farming should never be confused in this respect with dairy farming. It is conventional to say that the farmer owns the cows, but the unvarnished truth is that the cows own the farmer and are tyrannical about it to a degree that would appall the iron masters of nineteenth-century Birmingham. The dirt farmer, like the millionaire, has considerably greater freedom to set the time and duration of his vacation than does the wage earner who is given the last two weeks in July. With this proviso, one may say that Chautauqua exemplifies the native American type of vacation. One came to Chautauqua intent, for a precious interlude of innocent pretense, on being an Indian.

4. Sea Cybeles and salt water taffy

 The day came quickly enough when the vacation was its own excuse for being and no longer needed a noble motive. But somewhere in the land the noble motive must have been missing from the start, and when that place is found the birthplace of the vacation pure and simple has been located. As likely a locale as any is the sea coast of New Jersey. Certainly the vacation without extenuating circumstances took root there at a very early date.

Hardy pioneers summered without physiological or theological motives on the shore of Monmouth County directly after the American Revolution. An elderly lady of Long Branch sensed what this could mean and opened her home to summer renters. A Philadelphian in vigorous middle life further sensed that there was something very good indeed in her inspiration. He bought the house, rented rooms to the elite of Philadelphia, and died in fiscal comfort. In 1792 a Long Branch establishment advertised "a good stock of liquors and everything necessary for the entertainment of ladies and gentlemen," a mark of the vacation spirit if ever there was one. So blissful did it make the ladies and gentlemen that by 1806 the establishment had been expanded to take care of 250 of them.

Thus the summer hotel became an accomplished fact, accomplished without the aid of camp meetings and prayer and with only such increment to health as was consistent with a good stock of liquors and other patterns of entertainment. Technically it offered the vacation of the aristocrat, but the quite modest and unpretentious aristocrat without much lineage on which to lean and quite conscious that his castle rested almost literally on the sands. Furthermore he guarded the flank against the flesh and the devil by a set of blue laws adequate to protect the virtue which all concede to be a major Philadelphia achievement. Philadelphia opened Long Branch in one sense. New York would open it in the other.

We may now pass to the other end of the New Jersey coast and consider Cape May. The call of the siren was first heard from Cape May on June 30, 1801. Ellis Hughes was proprietor of the Hotel Atlantic. Cape May had had an economy of sorts, based on the whaling industry that had been imported from New England and Long Island. Mr. Hughes was enterprising enough to sense other possibilities, and therefore placed an advertisement in the Philadelphia *Daily Aurora*:

The public are respectfully informed that the subscriber has prepared himself for entertaining company who use sea bathing, and he is accommodated with extensive house room, with fish, oysters, crabs, and good liquors. Care will be taken of Gentlemen's horses.

The advertisement then continues in that modification of the dithyrambic mode suitable for advertisements in Philadelphia newspapers of the early nineteenth century, to praise the site of Cape May where Delaware Bay merges with the ocean, the entertainment that passing ships afford, the fact that carriages can be driven for miles upon the hard-packed sand, the easy slope that protects bathers from the danger of undertow, and most important of all to those who know what perspiration does to aspiration in the Philadelphia summer, "It is the most delightful spot a person can retire to in the hot season." Mr. Hughes added that the Cape May coach leaves Camden each Thursday, doing the 102 miles by Friday. There was the obvious rub, but it could be avoided. Those who prefer to sail, said the reassuring Mr. Hughes, "can find vessels almost any time."

A sloop began regular service between Philadelphia and Cape May in 1815; in 1816 the son of Ellis Hughes built the original Congress Hall Hotel; in 1819 steamboat service was inaugurated, and shortly thereafter Cape May was discov-

(above) *An 1880s boardwalk scene.*
(below) *Leland's Ocean Hotel, Long Branch, New Jersey.*

ered by those who fled the summer of Baltimore and
Washington, as well as Richmond and other cities with
limited summer delights farther south. Obviously the sort of
health that cooling summer breezes promotes was a magnet
drawing those in the fiscal position to be drawn to both Long
Branch and Cape May, but this is not quite the search for
health that brings the comfortably convalescent to a sulphur
springs. Similarly the blue laws that guarded virtue at Long
Branch and indeed at Cape May were designed to protect the
virtue already present rather than add to it. A summer
season at either place was a vacation and nothing else.

Between Long Branch, which is well within the New York
orbit, and Cape May, which is as far south as Washington, is
many a mile of sand beach and sand dune, inlet and tidal
river, salt water marsh and inland swamp, off-shore island
and shoal, and there are many, many miles of perfectly fine
locales for summer colonies. The nineteenth century was
well advanced before their development was practical. The
history of vacation can never be separated from the history
of travel, and for decades the practical way to the Jersey
shore was by boat and not by coach, whether from Camden
or anywhere else. There are those still ambulant who recall
the piers at Atlantic Highlands where summer steamers
daily disgorged their vacationists and even their commuters,
who would then be whisked to destination by Central of New
Jersey trains that panted close at hand. It is only ten miles
down the coast from Atlantic Highlands to Long Branch,
and there are a few points not far off the road from which
with binoculars one can sight the towers of Manhattan. The
practical way to Long Branch, with its good stock of liquors
and everything necessary for the entertainment of ladies
and gentlemen, long continued to be by boat. In similar
fashion Cape May is down the river and across the bay from
Philadelphia, and closer still to Wilmington, Delaware, a city
of reasonably easy access to Baltimore, Washington and
Richmond, as easy access was understood in the days when
the War of 1812 was a bitter Cape May memory. Vacation
started at Long Branch and Cape May partly because both
are fine vacation spots but mainly because each is easily

accessible by boat. This in turn necessitates a consideration of the State of New Jersey, and especially the State of New Jersey as it was when General Washington said his farewell to the armies at the Berrien Mansion at Rocky Hill, outside Princeton.

The 125 miles of coast between Long Branch and Cape May was a potential paradise of beaches, sand dunes, protected lagoons and other yachting waters. But it was far, far away as land travel was in those days when miles by stagecoach were truly miles. New Jersey is and has been from the start a state of fairly equal halves divided by a huge, teeming, roaring corridor. North and west of the New York-Philadelphia axis lies the pleasant, rolling countryside of north Jersey, rising to what by modest Jersey standards are mountains at the point where New Jersey blends with Pennsylvania and New York. South and east of the axis lies south Jersey, the great coastal plain that sinks and levels off into the pine barrens and then sinks even more into the swamps where the bog iron now rests unworked. But they were not pine barrens then. They were the great, primal, virgin forest of pine, cedar and oak. Here and there some pitiful scraps of forest have survived, to let the imaginative picture what that cathedral of the pines, the cedars and the oaks must have been before its rape was completed in 1860. It is the second growth that is the pine barrens, without economic value but very capable indeed of posing economic problems. Man, not nature, made so much of south Jersey next to worthless.

The New Jersey coast, then, was first probed from the north and the south where probing in the early nineteenth century was practical. As we have said, Long Branch and Cape May can be reached easily by boat, the one from New York and the other from Philadelphia, but the overland route to the mid-coast was through a primeval forest. The first objective of entrepreneurs, naturally, was the forest itself. The forest was systematically denuded in the first half of the century, and it takes more imagination than seventy miles an hour on the Atlantic City Expressway encourages to picture what that dreary right-of-way was like a century and a half ago. The best bet for one who wishes to see a fragment of the arboreal past is the Green Bank State Forest on the Mullica River, some fifteen miles north of the Egg Harbor City exit from the Expressway and light years away from it. The forest had to be penetrated before the beaches and sheltered inlets beyond could acquire economic practicality.

Deep in the forest were the swamps of south Jersey, and in the swamps bog iron. The Indians knew about the bog iron. Bog iron rust mixed with bear grease makes magnificent war paint. Iron masters of the modest sort that the economic possibilities of bog iron permit built their charcoal burning furnaces on the banks of the sluggish rivers that meander aimlessly through the flatlands of south Jersey. The rivers provided inexpensive but not particularly practical means of moving the iron, and the practicality was certainly not increased by the distance from the mouth of any one of them around Cape May to Philadelphia, or, if one preferred, around Sandy Hook to New York. There had to be a railroad, and in 1852 the Camden and Atlantic Railroad was started. In the genes of the C&A, which was built to haul bog iron from the swamps along with such fruit and vegetables as the land produced, were Atlantic City and all the lesser Atlantic Cities along the mid-coast of New Jersey. The high trees were quickly toppled and the bog iron soon lost out to iron mines and coal-burning smelters to the west, but Atlantic City was born. One may see a fragment of the metallurgical past at the Howell Works in Allaire State Park, off the Garden State Parkway, or the restored town of Batsto, east of the Hammonton exit from the Atlantic City Expressway. New Jersey is a dull state indeed at seventy miles an hour on either highway, but get off the highway, slow down to twenty miles an hour, or even to a walk, and an amazing amount of the dullness disappears.

The trees and the bog iron brought the railroad, and the railroad made possible Atlantic City. But first Atlantic City had to be a vision. This was the contribution of Dr. Jonathan Pitney. One day in May, 1820, Dr. Pitney came, for a reason seemingly lost in the fogs of Atlantic County antiquity, to

Hannah Holmes's tavern in Absecon. He even seems to have come by land, no insubstantial feat in itself. Few came to Absecon, and there were few reasons for coming there. One might dredge for oysters at Leed's Point or make salt on Absecon Island while waiting for the jetsam from one of the frequent wrecks. Detractors of Absecon, and they included nearly all who knew Absecon, maintained that an observer was stationed in the church belfry during services to watch for wrecks, lest the brigands of Brigantine forestall them. This may have been, although the further statement that in their piety the worshippers prayed for wrecks seems a canard.

But Dr. Pitney, whose shingle waved in the Absecon wind for half a century, saw health and happiness, and not impossibly wealth, in the magnificent beaches of the totally unpopulated island offshore. By 1852 the Camden and Atlantic had been started and his day had come. The offshore El Dorado was christened with quiet dignity Atlantic City, incorporation papers were signed on March 3, 1854, and two months later six-sevenths of the registered voters of Atlantic City, eighteen men to be exact, held the first city election. They dealt with realities: bathing regulations, liquor licenses, a jail and, as an afterthought, a school. On July 1, 1854, the first train rolled in from Camden with six hundred public and near-public figures on board. The bridge to the island was not finished, but they were rowed across. The United States Hotel was not finished, but they were fed. They viewed the sea and the sand, and they turned their eyes to the west, to far-off Absecon, and the depot, and the train beside it. They were safe in Camden before dark. On the Glorious Fourth the C&A was opened to all and sundry, who were free to taste the delights of Atlantic City. One delight was the gathering of seashells, another the clambering over old wrecks.

The future, however, belonged to Dr. Pitney and Atlantic City. Atlantic City has a magnificent beach and contemporary pollution itself can do little to its air. The coast curves in just the right way to shelter it from the worst of the northeasters and the Gulf Stream is never far off shore. Dr.

Some vacationers strolled, others rolled along in hired chairs on Atlantic City's boardwalk in the twenties.

Pitney was splendidly right, and what Atlantic City has become gloriously justifies his judgment. Whether he anticipated what it has become is another matter. He would seem to have been preoccupied with the scimitar curve of a beach, a southeast wind sweeping across from the Azores, a world where space is everywhere and time quietly fades out of thought. This is not precisely what Atlantic City has become.

It started with prophetic promptness to become what it is. The city was platted and its streets named for the seven seas, with Pacific Avenue outranking Atlantic just as the name Pacific outranks Atlantic in that other village with a global perspective, Nantucket. The Camden and Atlantic Land Company was formed and waterfront lots bought at $17.50 an acre in the pious expectation that the Atlantic City waterfront some day would sell at five hundred dollars an acre. In 1870 a local hotelman, Jacob Keim, and a C&A conductor, Alexander Boardman, looked at nature and were displeased. Nature is often cold and cloudy, and very often clammy and disagreeable. Nature should be methodized and improved, and the way to do it is to lay a boardwalk on the sand. One was laid that summer, eight feet wide. A boardwalk suggests a boardwalk ride, and in 1884 a Philadelphia maker of baby carriages and wheel chairs, M. D. Shill, brought his wares to the Atlantic City boardwalk. The latter were for cripples, but the real trade was to be with the vacationist turned aristocrat, enjoying nature methodized and improved as his faithful retainer braced himself and shoved.

In 1895 Mrs. Carl M. Voekler came home from a visit to Germany with a German idea, a postcard with a picture on it. Her husband, a printer, envisaged the picture postcard as an advertisement for hotels. It proved to be that and vastly more, and Atlantic City had another achievement to rank with the boardwalk and the perambulator for adults. There were left two other towering achievements, and by 1900 Atlantic City would be substantially what it is today. One was salt water taffy, which might be defined as highly elastic pulled candy made of sugar and molasses, capable of an infinitude of flavors and named for the Atlantic Ocean and not one of its ingredients. The other was the amusement pier, née 1882, which might in similar fashion be defined as a skyscraper lying on its side in the ocean with the sort of limited boardwalk frontage that the vertical skyscraper has on terra firma, but dedicated to pleasure, enlightenment and the sort of genial exploitation of human gullibility inseparable from places like Atlantic City.

Let us return to Long Branch and Cape May, and the beaches, dunes and inlets that lie between. By the day the train load of celebrities reached the rowboats to Atlantic City, its sea shells and half entombed wrecks, Long Branch had its hotels to rival Saratoga. Gone was the white flag, raised when ladies might bathe, and gone was the red flag that signalled all clear for gentlemen natators. Also gone was the wag who one day raised both flags simultaneously, with the havoc one may well imagine, and where he is gone one should not ask. Drinking and gambling profaned the landscape, the 1870 opening of the Monmouth Park race track helped little and the 1874 railroad from New York City not at all. By the 1880s Phil Daly was running his gambling club, and all the hymns Mrs. Daly and the ladies sang in the chapel in the Daly garden beyond did not necessarily divert the celestial attention from what Long Branch had become.

Celestial attention may have centered as well on Lillie Langtry and her private railroad car on the siding by the residence of her current uncle; on Diamond Jim Brady and Lillian Russell in their coupe which was thoughtfully lighted on the inside for the pleasure of the proletariat; or on Jim Fisk and his regiment drilling in their gold braids on the Bluff Parade Grounds. Perhaps it was just as well that Long Branch was discovered by the American presidency, and the stability high office connotes given to this giddy village by the sea. On a somber yet heart-warming note, the dying President Garfield was brought to Long Branch in 1881. To save him from the jolting carriage ride, the railroad workers and townfolk in a single night laid a half mile of track from the station to his cottage on Ocean Avenue. Garfield died at Long Branch. On the same Ocean Avenue where Garfield died, President Grant made his home the summer White

House. Presidents Hayes and Harrison were patrons of the old Elberon Hotel, and Woodrow Wilson had a home, Shadow Lawn, in West Long Branch. Presidents Grant, Hayes, McKinley, Arthur, Garfield and Wilson called the divine blessing on the land, themselves and possibly their respective parties at the gray Episcopal Church in the West End, later the Long Branch Historical Museum. To say that by 1900 Long Branch was what it is today would be unfair to 1900. It was vastly more.

The War of 1812 bore quite heavily on Cape May, as the natives waged a guerrilla warfare with the sailors of the blockading British fleet. The one redeeming feature of the conflict was that neither side descended to the use of firearms. The British, however, kept landing to replenish their water casks at Lilly Pond and to do a bit of extracurricular plundering of vegetable gardens. The natives retaliated by digging a ditch from the ocean to make the water of Lilly Pond saline and unsuitable. But skulduggery was nothing new to Cape May. Captain Kidd, whose penchant for landing along the Atlantic seaboard and burying treasure is well known, was pursued there in 1699. Since the treasure he buried has never been discovered, the digging for it is as good as ever and may properly be listed among the attractions of Cape May.

Once the war was safely over and visitors from Baltimore, Washington, Richmond and the steaming lands beyond discovered that there is nothing like water to the west with a southwest wind across it for keeping one cool in the summer, and Cape May is blessed with Delaware Bay in just the right position, the future was one of brilliant progress. Steamboat service, as we have said, was inaugurated and the number of summer visitors increased annually until, in 1853, a momentous decision was reached. Cape May was to have the largest hotel in the world. Builder Philip Cain erected a T-shaped summer palace three hundred feet wide in front and four stories high, with a wing at right angles five hundred feet long and three stories high. Even more impressive, and for that matter still impressive in the light of what older summer hotels still afford, each of the 482 rooms had a private bath. Fate allowed this crown jewel of the Jersey shore two years. It burned down on September 5, 1855.

Virtue faced its customary losing battle as the flower of the South and North alike poured into Cape May. Henry Cleveland's gambling house, the Blue Pig, was Cape May's very adequate answer to the challenge of Phil Daly's Long Branch establishment, but once more the presidency and near-presidency came to the rescue of Cape May and respectability. Henry Clay, mourning his son who was killed in the Mexican War, stayed at the Mansion House in 1847. Two years later "A. Lincoln and wife" registered there. Presidents Pierce and Buchanan arrived in 1855 and 1858 respectively, and President Grant in 1869. John T. Cunningham records in his *This Is New Jersey,* one of a series of books about Jersey that has made Mr. Cunningham the eminently readable historian of the state, its facts and foibles, that Mrs. Grant started a sewing spree on the Cape and the visiting belles madly sewed red and blue flannel bathing outfits, that they might follow the example, modest yet colorful, of the First Lady. But Fate was again to stalk the Cape as fires in 1869 and 1879 levelled much of the town.

The revival of Cape May was accomplished in a graceful fashion. The subdivision of Victorian architecture dedicated to summer dwellings by the sea flourished at Cape May and to this day the spacious, comfortable old houses built by carpenters with the instincts of artists are well preserved. Cape May has been blessed with the prime ingredient, a good summer climate. It has been blessed as well by relative inaccessibility. There was no decent road to Cape May until the Garden State Parkway was completed, and the ferry from Lewes, Delaware, which was proposed in 1900 and tried in 1903, did not become a fact until 1964. Finally, Cape May has been blessed by the fact that it has always drawn much of its clientele from the South. The mark of Southern graciousness, leisure and good taste rests like a benediction over Cape May. It is an old-fashioned place, quietly but resolutely old-fashioned.

Sheer numbers force us to pass over with silence or, at the most, brief mention the other fifty or so resort towns that are strung along the 120 miles of Jersey shore. It would be improper to pass over Ocean Grove and its wayward child Asbury Park. Ocean Grove is about ten miles down the coast from Long Branch and resolutely unassimilated with Asbury Park of which it might technically be called a suburb. Ocean Grove in its inception, and indeed today, offered the vacation as a by-product of the search for salvation after the Chautauqua fashion. In 1869 twenty persons pitched tent on the acres they had bought for fifty dollars. They were the forerunners of the Ocean Grove Camp Meeting Association. The Association so flourished that a decade after its formation it built an auditorium seating three thousand persons. No sooner was the Association formed than a brush manufacturer from New York, James A. Bradley, bought a vast seaside tract just north of the Grove. He envisaged a seaside resort for the respectable and God-fearing, attuned in spirit to Ocean Grove and resolutely defending the mores appropriate to it.

In the economic sense Asbury Park took off as though by jet propulsion, but it long stayed loyal to the ideals of its founder. By 1883 as many as 103 trains a day might pull through Asbury Park, but pull *through* they must on Sunday. No train might profane the Asbury Park Sabbath by stopping at the depot. The corollary where other forms of vice and folly are concerned need hardly be spelled out. Asbury Park has been quite thoroughly the victim of the day and age, but Ocean Grove most assuredly has not. There is still no vehicular traffic allowed in Ocean Grove from midnight Saturday to midnight Sunday, and the moralistic corollaries to that may be taken for granted. The writer finds this entirely admirable. Ours is a permissive society, and its hero is Henry David Thoreau who preferred swamps to dry land. A permissive society that idolizes Thoreau might conceivably rise to the nirvana of tolerance and understand a community that prefers Sabbath calm to Sabbath frenzy, and even respect the motive behind it. We tolerate everything else. We might well tolerate religious conviction.

Ocean Grove is the most notable but not the only Chautauqua to blend ocean breezes with the spirit of salvation along

the Jersey coast. Quakers from Philadelphia started Beach
Haven in 1870, Baptists founded Seaside Park in 1876, and
Methodists came to meeting at Island Heights in 1878. In
general, however, salvation has been a minor motive in the
establishment of Jersey resorts. Prohibition was long linked
with salvation in American minds, long before the link was
actually tested, and Ocean City was born bone dry in 1879.
Proximity to Atlantic City poses a perennial problem to
temperance, but Ocean City had a distraction. A Spanish
galleon laden with the silver of Peru rests on the bottom of
Great Egg Harbor, we are told, but like Captain Kidd's
treasure at Cape May, has not been found. Manasquan,
Beach Haven, Ventnor and by and large the rest have only
secular antecedents. Manasquan has memories of Robert
Louis Stevenson lying in bed on dark days at the old Union
Hotel and writing *The Master of Ballantrae*, and walking
abroad on bright days with his stepson Lloyd Osborne,
planning that final trip to the South Seas in search of the
elusive spirit of health which forever evaded him.

Such is the Jersey coast, and the time has come to be
philosophic about it. We return to our dogmatic and arbi-
trary premise, that the American vacation is formed after
one of two basic patterns. The New Jersey vacation is after
the pattern of the aristocrat. A pattern may be dominant
without being exclusive. We have seen the link between the
Indian pattern and the search for salvation as exemplified by
Chautauqua. The same link once led Ocean Grove to be called
Tent City, and obviously for the same reason. North Jersey
offers ample opportunities for those who would vacation
Indian fashion, and ample use is made of them. We hold
tenaciously, however, to our thesis where the Jersey shore is
concerned.

Each Jersey resort starts with a splendid beach. Rachel
Carson has pointed out that the east coast of America falls
into three sections: the rocky section down to Boston, the
sandy section from there to Florida, and the coral section
beyond. Rock begins to give way to sand at Old Orchard
Beach, Maine, but does not really yield to sand before
Plymouth, Massachusetts. Thereafter sand prevails, and the

Jersey shore is blessed with sand at its finest. But sand at its finest has never been good enough for New Jersey. Each Jersey resort must have its boardwalk. At first boardwalks were laid upon the sand; later they were elevated above it. The grandfather of boardwalks, the one at Atlantic City, is sixty feet wide, eight miles long, and, for practical purposes, is a street for pedestrians and vehicles propelled by man-power. What Atlantic City has in grandiose proportions, other Jersey resorts have in due proportions, and at some places due proportions approach grand. Thus at the Jersey beaches the vacationing aristocrat strides a surface that leaves his shine unaffected and the vacationing lady may don whatever footwear is at the moment appropriate for the de luxe approach to nature's simplicity.

A New Jersey beach is not thought perfected merely by the building of a boardwalk. One need not burrow in the sand at New Jersey, not with the cabana to cut off the east wind, the striped beach umbrella to suppress the sun, the beach chaise for extended comfort, and sometimes even the wooden platform resting on the sand for vacationing Ca-nutes. The Atlantic Ocean, of course, does pose a problem not simple of solution. The seaweed part is simple enough. Stranded seaweed can easily be raked up in the morning by young men of college age and aspirations. But the Atlantic Ocean is quite capable of being cold and choppy, to the point of being disagreeable. The logical way to improve and methodize the Atlantic is to draw salt water toward the hotel or motel pool into which after appropriate filtering and with the aid of adequate warming it may be allowed to enter and be enjoyed by the lords and ladies taking the waters at the Jersey shore.

Atlantic City has been called many things but not Tent City, nor has any other Jersey resort. In New Jersey one expects the hotel or motel to have a private balcony for each room as well as an enclosed pool for the visiting courtiers. A little dexterity may let one come up with a room that has a private refrigerator. A modicum of wisdom will lead one to select an establishment with a sundeck where one may sit out swaddled mummy fashion when the wind is chill but the sunshine strong, the air invigorating, and Nature herself somehow penetrating the improvements. One expects a good dining room, with a menu artfully printed with detailed reference to the bounty of the field and the stream but with a cuisine supremely inappropriate to the simple life beside either. One expects the range of additives to whisky, gin and rum that effect the array of cocktails marshalled on the document known by respected American tradition as the wine list. One expects on-premises parking for one's car, or attendant parking for it if the premises are inadequate. One expects all this, and a stiff bill for it, for all this is what a lord and his lady have a right to expect, and the Jersey shore specializes in lordly vacations.

There are those who sneer at vacation on the Jersey shore and places of its sort. The sneer is most frequent on the faces of the supercilious and sophisticated who delight in the abstract thought of natural simplicity. We have a generation with us that plays at being peasants and milkmaids in their way just as truly as did the lords and ladies of eighteenth-century Versailles in theirs. Our wandering minstrels with their guitars and horizontal thumbs found on every roadside and at the entrance to every limited access highway usually are subsidized by parents, and not infrequently by grants from the federal government. Those who play at being tramps have no right to scoff at those who play at being lords. The subsidized young man who rolls up in his sleeping bag twenty feet off the highway is play-acting at being a tramp. Why should he scoff at the man who takes his ease at his own expense in a luxury hotel, play-acting at being an aristocrat? The state of each is a happy state, so long as it is solidly grounded on pretense. One might ask the real lord if his state is invariably one of wine and roses. Or, for that matter, one might ask the real tramp.

So, at the Jersey shore one pretends to be a lord. A wooden pavement is laid upon the sand, a shelter is provided against the rude, unmannerly wind, castle after castle awaits the approval and the patronage of the visiting lord and lady, and they dine as the aristocracy never dined in any castle by the storied Rhine. Let one who has never vacationed by the

Jersey shore refrain from scoffing, for one who has vacationed there will certainly not do so. But in this, as in all the good things of life, prudent and thoughtful selectivity are needed for the best results. One suggestion is a week in April when there is heat in the sun and cold in the air, an Atlantic City hotel with a sundeck, reclining chairs into which milord and his lady have been wrapped like twin cocoons, and a wise passivity assumed as nature seeps through every pore, and health can be felt coursing through every vein. Perhaps it is a mirage, April weather being what it usually is, but a mirage is the pretense of something real and substantial, and sometimes one is lucky and pretense becomes reality.

Perhaps Atlantic City is best as a mirage. Time was when it made a magnificent mirage, in the days when the Merchant and Miner line boats made the journey from Boston to Philadelphia a delight, and not the boredom it is by plane, the ordeal it is by train, or the horror it is by auto. It took twenty-four hours or more, and every minute could be golden. If one was fortunate enough to pass in daylight hours, Atlantic City looked like "a sea Cybele fresh from Ocean, Rising with her tiara of proud towers." One sat on deck and watched Atlantic City unroll, striving to identify the hotels and piers. Distance, the lacy haze, sunlight caroming off the waves, all combined to make Atlantic City a Camelot by the sea, a magic city of knights and gentle ladies, and deeds of brave renown. That it was nothing of the sort made no difference. Nothing real should make a difference when you are on vacation. Probably Atlantic City is still Camelot, if only one could see it from the deck of a comfortable coastal steamer.

5. *Fun city*, 1920

We said at the outset that our focal point would have
to be the city of Boston and whatever radiated from it by
way of vacation, and this for the unassailable good reason
that it was the writer's personal focal point and it was along
the radii from that center that he traveled. It has been our
purpose to this point to establish obliquely that there was
nothing unique about that focal point, and certainly its radii
did not travel into the undiscovered. There were Saratogas
in New England, and there were Chautauquas. Above all,
there was and is a Jersey shore. Certain patterns of vacation
became established, accepted and perpetuated in places like
Saratoga, Chautauqua and Atlantic City. Their counterparts
came into being elsewhere, in some places no doubt by way
of conscious imitation but in far more places through the
fact that vacation spots come into being through a sort of
spontaneous generation where topography, climate, accessi-
bility and potential business come harmoniously together.
They certainly do so in New England, on the coast of five
states, in the mountains of three states and the mini-moun-
tains of two others, and by the lakes of all six. But there was
another place where they were once harmoniously present,
and that was the city.

One of the tragic truths of contemporary life is the fact
that the American city has all but ceased to be a vacation
place. We go to see London, Paris, Rome, Vienna, Madrid.
Fewer and fewer go to see even Washington and New York,
and cities like Boston, Chicago, St. Louis, not to mention
New Orleans and San Francisco, have dwindled as vacation
objectives. The mayor of New York in as pathetic an attempt
to recapture a destroyed past as recent history records,

attempted to christen New York, Fun City. There was a time when New York and many other cities were fun, fun as travel objectives and fun as places in which to live. What is more, in days when the vacation was by no means as nearly universal as it is today and when even the single day snatched from the workaday pattern and dedicated to sheer enjoyment was a pearl beyond price and people were as determined as Browning's little mill worker Pippa not to "squander a wavelet of thee, A mite of my twelve-hours' treasure," even the city where one lived was a prime vacation place.

There was a time when Boston was fun. Cities are really for the young to enjoy, not the children but those who have reached the freedom of adulthood without life yet having closed in upon them. There are a few precious years in which young adulthood has a sense of permanence. It passes, to be sure, but it is precious even in retrospect. It is doubly and trebly precious when it is shared, lover with lover, husband with wife, parents with children. Our present concern is mainly with the third category, since a half century ago vacation for many was not a stretch of days but that momentary break with the workaday world, that momentary venture into the world of pleasure for the parents, of wonder and delight for the children.

In its simplest and in some respects its purest form it came on the day when a young mother saw that the sky was blue, the air was clear and the outdoors beckoning. This was the day the Lord made for the swanboat. West of Boston's historic and dishevelled Common is a meticulously manicured stretch of greenery called the Public Garden. Walks edged with pebbles that match neatly in size wind in lazy serpentine fashion around large and comfortable trees with arms that spread out benevolently and drop cool shade upon benches beneath. Beside the walks are flower beds that some spring morning miraculously bring forth perfectly formed and perfectly matched tulips, and repeat thereafter the miracle with flowers appropriate to the season until winter calls quietus. Down the middle of the Garden is its one cement walk, leading from the street that divides the

Common from the Garden, bridging the lagoon which is the Garden's central and dominating feature, passing the statue of George Washington who benevolently views the Back Bay he won for his country that St. Patrick's Day on Dorchester Heights, crossing another street to become a tree embowered walk by the stately boulevard that divides Commonwealth Avenue, where Brahmins once strolled and Brahmin children sedately played and now scholars in rented residence en route to careers as auto mechanics, paramedical technicians, airplane hostesses and hairdressers find boisterous relaxation.

We passed the swanboats on our way west. In the lagoon is a fleet surely unique in maritime history. A swanboat is a broad, flat-bottomed craft with seats across the ship designed to hold five or six squealing children with a parent at each end as a stopper. At the rear is a massive swan, facing left and right in feathered white perfection and separated in

Swan boat on the lake in the Public Garden, Boston.

the middle by a seat. The seat is occupied by a young man working his way through college by propelling the swanboat bicycle fashion, the pedals attached to paddles that move the swanboat forward with all the dignity, slowness and majestic calm of the swan itself. Not a ripple ruffles the water in front of the swanboat, not the trace of a wake follows it astern, as it makes its leisurely way over a course it has followed for nearly one hundred years, toward the Boylston Street side of the Garden, around the tiny island, back under the bridge, toward the Beacon Street side of the lagoon, around the other island in a spacious arc, and back to the tiny wharf where another contingent of children with parents as seat stoppers awaits it impatiently, as the parents did when they were children, and their parents when they were children, and so back to 1877 when the first swanboat was launched in the Public Garden. The day that the children were taken in town to ride on the swanboat was a red letter vacation day fifty years ago, and indeed a hundred years ago, and blessedly still is today. The swanboat was and is Fun City at its innocent childhood best.

The swanboat is unique, but Franklin Park is not. Every city has Franklin Park under one name or another, and it is a fortunate city that has kept it in the innocence and safety of fifty years ago. Boston's Franklin Park had an approach worthy of its delights. Columbia Road, which made its leisurely way upward from the plebian and mercantile precincts of Uphams Corner to the sylvan delights that crowned the rise, was then no ordinary thoroughfare. A city, wise to the needs of all its residents, paved the left side of the road for motorized traffic but kept the right side in carefully groomed earth for the carriages of those who drove on Sunday afternoon from Commonwealth Avenue for an airing in the Park. For those whose economic status entitled them to a place in neither the motorized traffic nor the carriage trade, there was the streetcar. In summer it was a streetcar with a difference. The open car was in design not entirely different from the swanboat, with the obvious exception of motor power. Seats ran across the car, each seat being entered by ascending a two-step running board that ran along both sides of the car. A protective bar was dropped across the left side of the car where cars on the other track posed an obvious danger, but the right side was the free side. Young bloods rode on the running board with studied disdain of the car's lurching and jolting, and conductors blessed with great dexterity and length of arm somehow swung around them as they worked up and down the car collecting fares. It was a point of honor with all able-bodied men to swing off the car before it stopped. A ride in the open car was a fitting prelude to the delights of Franklin Park, and the ride back an appropriate finale to its pleasures.

The fundamentals of the Park were the zoo, the picnic areas, the miniature and rather remote lagoon and the walks. As time went on there were added the golf course and the lawn tennis courts, but they lie outside the scope of this study. The zoo was routine enough although more than satisfying to its youthful devotees. The highlight was the Saturday afternoon performance of three elephants named Mollie, Waddie and Tony, who sat on stools, talked to one another on the telephone, did a partial approximation of a piggyback ride, and in other ways demonstrated that with adequate drillwork of sufficient intensity the stupidest elephant can be made to learn the fundamentals of knowledge. This was also the educational philosophy of the day for young humanity. The other animals were just to look at. There were the lazy lion, the restless tiger, the raccoons who were always washing things in their pathological dedication to cleanliness, and a whole aviary of highly improbable-looking birds. Zookeeping had not yet developed into a science. Obviously someone knew how to take care of the animals, since the same animals were there year after year, but one imagines that most of the subsidiary positions went to those deserving of political largesse.

Picnics are among the least changing of all human activities, and the resemblance of the picnic of half a century ago to the picnic of today was enhanced by the presence of what fifty years ago was a recent and invaluable invention, the thermos bottle. Actually an array of thermos bottles was required for a picnic of any substantial size. There was the thermos of milk for the children. For the adults the thermos might contain such a Boston favorite as Moxie, or possibly root beer or golden ginger ale. Coca-Cola found the going slower north of Long Island Sound, although New England is long since captive territory. We might pause at this point for a touch of philology. Strangers are puzzled to the point of bafflement by the fact that soft drinks, known collectively elsewhere as *pop*, around Boston are called *tonic*. Ginger ale is tonic, Coca-Cola is tonic and so is Seven-Up. Local philologists trace this bit of local semantics back to the fact that Moxie was first introduced as a health-building tonic, won far more adherents by its pleasant taste than by its health-promoting qualities, and once management discovered that the gratifying multitude who were ordering Moxie at the drug store were drinking it as a beverage, Moxie ceased to be a tonic and became a soft drink obtainable at a general store. It continued to be tonic, however; in general parlance and by analogy so did all the other soft drinks, and tonic they are in Boston to this day.

Then in the 1920s there was the other thermos from which the children were barred and which was handled with a touch of furtiveness that was a stimulus in itself. It was the period of the national aberration called Prohibition. Prohibition to some extent ruffled the tranquillity of even the Boston scene. It certainly upset the economics of the local liquor trade, increasing substantially the price of hard liquor and decreasing in equal measure its reliability. It might be plausibly argued that Prohibition aided sobriety, since Canadian ale from the easily accessible oases north of the border was a more practical medium for rum-running than the very much more expensive hard liquors, and although Canadian ale has never been lacking in alcoholic authority, it is very much less than that of whiskey. On the other hand Prohibition rather aided the spirit of intimacy which is so strong an element in conviviality. There was a snug seclusion to a properly operated speakeasy that was attractive in itself, and although the link between Prohibition and organized crime started a cancerous growth in American society that has never been excised, such sociological problems were no concern of those who knocked three times and asked for Joe. Accompanied by wife and children and two neighbors with their wives and children all on safari in Franklin Park, husbands found vast contentment and ease of spirit in that other thermos, and the spirit of vacation for that short but blessed day rested on them.

Boston has other areas that made suitable one-day vacation sites but let us turn to two havens of happiness outside the city, the two major beaches with which Greater Boston is blessed, Revere Beach to the north or perhaps rather to the east, and Nantasket Beach to the south. Both are magnificent stretches of sand, more than verifying Rachel Carson's thesis that the rock ends at Boston and the sand begins.

Indeed half the fun was getting there where Revere Beach was concerned. It cannot be at the outside more than ten miles from downtown Boston to Revere Beach, yet for a great majority of Bostonians getting to Revere Beach entailed travel on every form of mechanized transportation available in the first quarter of the twentieth century. You took the streetcar in town from wherever you lived. Boston was honeycombed with streetcar lines at that period, and a great many of them terminated in endless crawls up the narrow streets of what we are now supposed to call the inner city. Likely as not the streetcar brought you to the South Station, the larger of the two railroad termini of the city and Boston's gateway to the south and west. Above the South Station were the Forest Hills–Sullivan Square elevated train tracks. One left the streetcar, climbed the stairs, gave the lady in the booth one's transfer, and boarded the train for the ride to the ferry slip. The distance was short and one could reach it on foot almost as quickly as by elevated train, but there was no reason to diminish one's delight and besides, you must not waste your transfer. At the slip one boarded the ferry for the ride across Boston Harbor to East Boston. Exhilarated by this, one was ready for the best, which lay ahead. It was the ride on the narrow gauge train which manfully chugged away from the wharf at East Boston on its way to Winthrop, to far away Lynn, but also to Revere Beach itself. Streetcar, elevated train, ferry and

A summer excursion. Band members occupy first row of trolley seats.

steam train, and all for twenty-five cents or so. What modern airline, emblazoning a newspaper page with calls to far-off lands and distant ports, and boasting of barely subsonic speed and certainly supersonic comfort enroute, can offer as much as this, in so short a time, at so small a cost?

There loomed ahead the Thunderbolt, the Derby Racer, the shooting galleries with ducks that majestically and endlessly floated from right to left, sinking like the sun momentarily to rise again. There was the gloriously gaudy facade beneath which creamy frozen custard emerged in mounting spirals that rose higher and higher above the flatbottom ice cream cone until it seemed inevitable that gravitation would call a halt to glory but somehow never did. For those of more tender years than befitted a roller coaster there was the merry-go-round, with horses that rose and fell in rhythmic and symmetrical gallop as a more than adequate head of steam made the calliope bray and as mother rode in an ornate coach seat beside the horse and held out a profoundly resented protective hand toward the equestrian. There was even something for father as well, if he was a gaming man as he tended to be and if he felt that merry-go-rounds were outside his province as he surely did. He and his ilk could stand at the base of the Derby Racer and bet on the cars. Two cars started simultaneously on separate tracks of meticulously equal length that rose and fell separately, interweaving but never intersecting. Eventually the two cars would roar toward the finish line, and one would beat the other by the breadth of a hair. There was absolutely no way that the result of their race could be predicted, no way it could be fixed. The odds on the cars were always even, and there was universal agreement that over the summer one car won as often as the other.

With all these glories west of the Boulevard it seems almost an anticlimax to say that the Atlantic Ocean lay to the east. Yet the ocean also had its lure, and there were times when the conflicting tug of what God had wrought and what man had embellished it with were physically painful. There were, however, the beach, and the lunch on the beach, and the swim in the waters of Revere which were chill enough for the hardiest but never had the arctic quality of waters farther north. There was a ritual to be observed in all these matters. It was the universal belief, possibly pure science and possibly pure folklore, that one could not go into the water until an hour after eating. The problem in logistics was by no means of simple solution, since many discordant factors had to be resolved. When do we swim? When do we eat? Do we swim before we eat? If we eat first, what do we do before we swim? When do we go on the merry-go-round, or the roller coaster, or venture heart-in-mouth through the House of Horrors? Can we shoot at the ducks in the shooting gallery? Why not? Why doesn't dad ride on the Derby Racer instead of just watching it? Yet always the logistics were resolved, everything was fitted in, the most reluctant accepted the fact that the sun had sunk behind the Derby Racer as proof that the day was about done, and besides a fair fraction of the fun was the return trip. Ahead was the ride on the narrow gauge train, the ride on the boat, the ride on the elevated train, and if luck was with us the ride on an open car. The spirit of vacation also rested on a day at Revere Beach and if a day of anxious waiting can be like a year, a year of happiness can be crammed into such a day as the day at Revere Beach when children are young and, for that matter, so are their parents.

Nantasket Beach rose a notch or two above Revere Beach on the social scale. There was more than a single factor involved in its superior distinction. Probably the most important one was the fact that a large part of Nantasket Beach was given over to summer cottages, and the best of them rather elegant. Thus the proportion of honky-tonkdom to residential stability was lower at Nantasket than at Revere. An equally important factor might have been that Nantasket was farther away and took a much longer boat ride. Nantasket Beach is the outer edge of a narrow, elongated, curving peninsula that leaves the mainland at Hingham, turns back upon itself, and almost returns to Boston before it runs out of sand. It can be reached by road and was by the affluent who owned automobiles, but the one right way of going to Nantasket was by boat, and for that matter still is. Since the Nantasket peninsula cooperates so splendidly, the boat ride took hardly more time than the auto ride, if indeed as much. Its prelude was the same as that of Revere Beach since the Nantasket boat left from a wharf near the ferry slip, but there resemblance ended. The Nantasket boat gave you a real ride down the harbor, not a tantalizing taste as did the East Boston ferry. Boston has an attractive island-studded harbor and it is not a childhood illusion that has gathered glamor with the passing years which makes the ride to Nantasket a remembered delight. It really is a very pleasant hour afloat, and those highly intelligent fathers who parked their families at Nantasket for the summer and commuted to Boston daily by boat had commuting at its superb best.

Probably the superiority of Nantasket to Revere would not stand the test by qualitative analysis, once the matter of residential property was conceded. It had about the same kind of amusements and of about the same quality. It did have in Paragon Park a cluster of seaside delights like a tunnel of love and a house of horrors, but they were available as individual enterprises at Revere. The state did erect a capacious if rather formal pavilion at the land edge of the sand where the more sedate visitors whose years did not suggest the informality of sitting on the sand might relax, enjoy the sea breeze and avoid the sun. The sand at Nantasket was superb, but so was the sand at Revere. One falls back upon the thought that distance can lend enchantment not only in prospect but also in realization. How else can one explain the undoubted fact that a person is far more apt to have the experiences conventional to the distant places than the similar experiences close to home? The suggestion for what it is worth is that Nantasket was better than Revere because it was farther away and cost more to get to. It is a mistake to think that grass is greener in the distant pasture only when seen from a distance. It is actually greener when you get there. Otherwise, how do you justify the journey?

The thought of the Nantasket boat brings to mind the thought of the Plymouth boat, and the Provincetown boat.

One of the great losses Boston has suffered in these more recent years, in which loss and not gain has been the universal urban experience, has been the loss of the Atlantic Ocean. The ocean is still there, but it is not used the way it once was for vacation purposes. Time was, and we must return shortly to that time in this chronicle, when one could sail as a passenger from Boston to more ports than space and time are available to enumerate. Two of them, Plymouth and Provincetown, provided two of the finest one-day outings ever enjoyed by mortal man. Plymouth was the more educational of the two, but the boat ride was an hour shorter. Possibly balanced against this was the fact that the Plymouth boat hugged the South Shore, whereas the Provincetown boat put boldly out to sea. You saw more from the Plymouth boat, but had a greater spirit of adventure on the Provincetown boat.

Plymouth was unquestionably the more educational but this seems in retrospect to have been considered an advantage chiefly by parents to whom education can be an obsession. Their offspring could look at Plymouth Rock. Plymouth Rock gives the visitor instantaneous and total self-revelation, but nothing else. There is nothing you can do to Plymouth Rock except look at it, and that does not take long. The Pilgrim museum in Pilgrim Hall offered more, but not necessarily more of interest to children nor is it entirely clear that the education of a person of any age is necessarily advanced by viewing antiquities unless he has a good prior schooling in antiquarianism. Actually the visitor to Plymouth today, be he young or old, is in far better shape than one was fifty years ago because now he can grope his way around a fine replica of the *Mayflower* and he can watch the past self-consciously recreated by craftsmen playing at work on that fine reproduction of Massachusetts antiquity, Plimoth Plantation. But he cannot go to Plymouth by boat, unless he owns the boat himself. That is the tragedy of it all. The best part of the Plymouth trip always was the boat ride down and back. That was better even than the shore dinner.

Provincetown, on the other hand, was and is a nautical goal worthy in itself. In the first place there is the main street which is incredibly narrow, even by the austere standards of downtown Boston. There was something at which to gape, in the days when culture was just beginning to percolate through Provincetown, when some strange appearing persons identified in a whisper as artists could be seen and discreetly gawked at in the way appropriate to life of a different order from one's own. Then there was the climb up the steep hill and the far more rigorous climb up the Pilgrim Memorial Monument, the Italian bell tower that crowns the hill and commemorates in architectural terms appropriate to Florence or Siena the fact that the Pilgrims paused at Provincetown before they proceeded to Plymouth. The architecture of the Monument never bothered us, for who had ever heard of Florence or Siena, nor does it bother visitors today half as much as the steepness and the height.

Provincetown posed one grave question: Should one take a precious hour from one's time on land for a shore dinner or should a hastily gobbled Hershey bar suffice until the fleshpots of the ship's lunch counter once more were available, so that the time thus saved could be devoted to a ramble about Provincetown? The second answer was, of course, the right one, but the restaurants of Provincetown did their advertising mightiest to keep it from being the inevitable one. Provincetown had one estimable advantage over Plymouth. Provincetown, like the rest of Cape Cod, has absolutely nothing educational about it except, of course, the environmental lecture now given at the nearby National Seashore Park and the very important oceanographic work done at the other end of the Cape, at Woods Hole. A half century ago there was no Seashore Park and the latter is by its nature only for those of highly specialized erudition. The result of Provincetown's blessed freedom from anything important enough in its past to be called history was that there was nothing to do at Provincetown except enjoy it. Provincetown was worthy of the ride down and back, and praise can go no higher. Not everything of value in Massachusetts has been lost. You can still go to Provincetown by boat.

History and the educational have always been part of the glory of Greater Boston, and also part of the problem. The glory stays fairly static, the problem far less so. At the best the problem is endemic. It can mount to the epidemic stage, and as the 1960s proved it is capable of crises. The fusion of history and the educational with vacation has posed a particular problem of its own, especially for the young. It is the viewpoint of the young that for a moment we shall attempt to recapture. Because Greater Boston fairly reeks with history, it drips with opportunities for education. Bunker Hill is a case in point. Bostonians and especially those who live in Charlestown where the Monument is located tend to view the Bunker Hill Monument with experienced disdain. Outlanders might toil up its endless steps and be rewarded with the view of Charlestown, the Mystic River, the less than lordly reaches of Chelsea and from a different angle Boston itself, a red brick city when seen from such an eminence. This was learned from veterans of the climb, mainly visitors from distant parts. The native of Charlestown had the indifference toward the Monument that dwellers in the west of Ireland have toward salt water bathing or, one imagines, natives of Tibet have toward mountain climbing.

Of the educational opportunities, far and away the best was the *U.S.S. Constitution*. Old Ironsides is a glorious vessel of oak and cedar, full of entrancing nooks and crannies, and delightfully narrow passageways. The fact that it is historic and educational made not the slightest difference; it was a glorious take-in despite such handicaps. Paul Revere's house ranked high as well. It was very different from the houses to which the average Bostonians were accustomed, even from the houses of Charlestown and other sections which were never thought of as the inner city, houses that never embodied the latest thought in domestic architecture. There was also something to be said for Faneuil Hall, although the young visitor was less preoccupied with its glory as Cradle of Liberty than with its excitement on the lower level where the liveliest commerce in fruit and vegetables took place. Something, but not much, could also be said for the Old North Church.

Once you left Boston proper, however, things shelved off

sharply. Cambridge had Longfellow's house, which offered little to youth except a vetoed suggestion about playing catch on the open park area across the street. Concord was considerably worse. One had been told that Longfellow was a poet, which no doubt explained his living in a dignified but dull house. Emerson, on the other hand, was not even a poet and yet his Concord house was dull. Concord had the house where Louisa May Alcott lived, but she wrote girls' books. There was the rude bridge that arched the flood, but the bridge wasn't rude and that was certainly no flood beneath it. All in all, in spite of the ride on the open car from where the subway ended at Harvard Square out the leisurely stretches to Arlington Square and then by some now forgotten mode of travel—probably a steam train—to Lexington and then to Concord, historic and educational Massachusetts was a pretty dull affair. It was considered important, however, and one was taken over the course. Even from the vantage point of years that brings greater respect for history and education, the impression of dullness does not entirely disappear although nothing dispels dullness so effectively as knowledge. Dull or not, the tour of historic and cultural Massachusetts is a convenient courtesy device toward visitors from foreign parts, constructive and informative, and capable of killing a day. Bostonians still subject visitors from Minnesota, Iowa and other lands unhymned by Longfellow and unphilosophized by Emerson to the full Greater Boston historic and educational treatment. If they return to their native acres better reconciled to their cornfields and their hog pens, the modest purpose of their host is fulfilled. They have seen historic and educational Boston, and they will never have to do that again.

There lay ahead for the one-day outing a prodigious expansion, once the automobile became more than the cherished possession of the affluent few. That is so obviously a subject in itself, and its ramifications so thick and thorny, that it could never be appended as a coda to a chapter dealing in the main with such pleasant simplicities as a ride on the swanboat or a day in Franklin Park. Besides, to consider the gradually unfolding potentialities of the auto as a pleasure vehicle in a chapter devoted to such around-the-corner localities as Revere and Nantasket beaches, or even such hinterland Edens as Plymouth and Provincetown, would be to cloud the essential significance of what the one-day outing was a half century ago. In 1924 Boston and its immediate environs were full of places to which mothers could take children for weekday outings and where whole families could enjoy a Sunday holiday, previously unmentioned places like Norumbega Park, Spot Pond, the Blue Hills, the Strandway, Wollaston Beach and many more besides. Some of them are as available today as they ever were, as are some of those we have described in detail. Some of them are available with an element of danger, and some are unavailable because of the constant presence of danger.

The one group in American society today which has attained in its perfection that indifference to race, creed and color which liberals acclaim to be the goal of American society is the criminal class. They inflict violence without the slightest regard to race, creed or color. The result is that peaceful Bostonians of every race, creed and color do their best to avoid places in which violence is an unremitting peril, and places that once were oases of peace now are deserts of ominous quiet. The reader may draw the parallels appropriate to his own city, and there is not a large city in America for which they cannot be drawn.

Naturally we did not know that we were in a Golden Age half a century ago, but we did at least suspect that we were in a good time in which to live. Most of us were close enough to European patterns of living to know that we or our forebears had bettered themselves by coming to America. There was enough evidence of progress in the physical realm to show that we lived more comfortable lives than had our grandparents, and enough evidence of economic progress to show that we were better off than they. We certainly looked back with envious desire upon the 1920s when we were bemired in the 1930s and the 1940s. The decade that started in 1950 stood comparison fairly well with the decade that started in 1920, but thereafter the record needs no comment. It certainly needs no comment where cities are concerned.

Perhaps the Golden Age cannot be recaptured, but it can be consciously imitated. Half a century ago family ties were far closer than today, pleasures enjoyed far more by family units. There was often a basic simplicity to such enjoyment, and very simple places like the Boston Public Garden or Franklin Park, Revere Beach or Nantasket Beach were often the locales. One of the encouraging signs today is the way that many young people are simplifying their lives, turning back to nature and the natural, finding that the satisfaction a pleasant experience gives and the price tag on it may be entirely unrelated. We knew that half a century ago, not all of us to be sure and none of us all the time but enough of us to keep the beach crowded at Revere and the boats running to Nantasket. It may well be that recollections of rides on the swanboat and picnics at Franklin Park have a more basic justification than the pleasant recollection of things past. Unless one is entirely a pessimist, there is a corner of his mind that lodges an important thought. The Golden Age did not just happen. Greeks made it happen for some precious decades in ancient Athens, Romans for many decades in ancient Rome. The people of Florence made it happen in their day, as the people of Venice in theirs. Paris once was the capital of the civilized world, and London somehow has never ceased to be a great city as well as a huge one. City names like Salzburg and Vienna make the mind tingle. Cities have had their Golden Age, all right, and American cities have had theirs. But the Golden Age has never been exclusively one of awe-inspiring, creative accomplishments. It has been as well the creation of people living the good life in the harmony of law and order, and very often the good life was simple indeed. The good life was simple in the best form it took in the American cities half a century ago, and it never took a better form than the one-day outing at a local beach or park.

6. South of Boston

 No matter how glorious a day of total freedom in the city or the city outskirts may have been, a day is not a vacation. We have contracted far enough. Now it is time to expand again and consider the vacation areas easily accessible to Boston half a century ago and utilized to the practical full by vacationing Bostonians. Perhaps a touch of pedantry will be permitted. East of Boston is the Atlantic Ocean, and we shall return to it when we reach the steamship. North of Boston are the states of Maine and New Hampshire, and we shall let Maine do service for its neighbor to the west. No matter what the compass or the geography book says, Vermont is north of New York, not north of Boston, and in terms of vacation there is no West of Boston until you reach the Far West. Once you get far enough west of Boston to reach a Massachusetts vacation area, you are out of the Boston orbit and in the orbit of New York. The Berkshires are in Massachusetts and the Green Mountains are in Vermont, but for vacation purposes they belong to New York and New Jersey. There remains a pleasant land south of Boston, a land with no annals except in Plymouth, no poet to rhapsodize about it as Robert Frost has done for New Hampshire and no painter to limn its charm as Andrew Wyeth has for way down Maine. And yet the South Shore, like Cape Cod beyond it, was a wonderfully accessible and satisfying vacation land in the pleasant days when the war to end wars had been won, the consulship of Calvin Coolidge was at high noon, the federal budget was about what the New York City budget is today, and the income tax was to the average man a cloud on the distant horizon no larger than his hand. Let us move South of Boston.

Boston was blessed a half century ago by three railroads and two railroad stations. At the hour of writing one of the latter is crumbling beneath the demolition ball and the other is the darkened abode of bats and crawling creatures. This statement, we hasten to add, is based even more on imagination than hearsay, since the writer certainly has not been in the North Station since Hector emerged from pupdom nor has he talked with anyone who has of late penetrated its fastnesses. We suspect, however, that it is not inaccurate. There is precious little railroading north of Boston today, and waiting accommodations on what exists are decidedly al fresco.

The station now passing into memory was the South Station, and it was a terminal in the strict sense of the word. Boston, like Chicago, was a city through which no passenger train ever passed. Not even New York had that distinction. The station had a great rotunda facing business Boston, and through its portals human hordes poured out in the morning and in at evening, in the undeviating tidal action of the world of commerce and industry. Inside was a great arcade. To the left were the ticket windows for those whose ventures into the world of travel were to be modest, not transcending the trackage of the two railroads the station served. To the right were the tracks, over twenty of them, with the gates closed or opened by functionaries of great dignity but somewhat threadbare uniform. As trains were slowly backed in, their itineraries were unrolled in some mysterious fashion and duly posted, and their passengers entered in a range of gaits that extended from the leisurely stroll of the seasoned drummer to the nervous trot of the vacationer who was sure that a train with 600 seats would never accommodate the fifty early birds already waiting for its arrival. There were kiosks midway in the rotunda. One was for the high priests of railroading who could map one's course with practiced ease to the Ultima Thule of the railroad world, or flip without looking the proper local table to the person whose aspirations extended no farther than Canton Junction. Another kiosk was reserved for the merchandising of the essentials of railroad travel: the six newspapers then pub-

South Station, Boston—jumping-off place for many an East Coast adventure.

lished in Boston, the *Saturday Evening Post* and its compeers, the Hershey bar and its competition, and as time went on the paperback book. Other kiosks in increasing numbers were devoted to the sale of bakery products and other wares invaluable to the commuter with limited culinary opportunities. Such kiosks diluted the sanctity of the rotunda in the mind of railroad buffs, but doubtless helped with the taxes.

The great glory of the South Station was the Waiting Room. This was a regal hall, indeed worthy of a king in residence and not beneath the dignity of an imperial coronation. The walls were tiled, and the South Station was built in a day when ceramic tile had no competition. The tiles were dirty, but this was a day when soot was merely soot and not pollution. The seats were massive benches of stout oak, with backs that soared majestically and then gracefully rounded off. They were never built for mortals. One can picture Michelangelo's Moses seated on a bench in the South

Station and not dwarfed by it, but hardly a human being. Above each bench was the name of a Massachusetts county, a form of immortality that in a sense paid off. There is no state in the union in which counties mean less than in Massachusetts, where they exist chiefly for the benefit of the politically faithful, and rare indeed is the Bay State bird who could name even a few of them. In those days, however, one could agree to meet a friend in Hampden, Middlesex or Barnstable and at least know that these were counties, even if one was vague as to where they were.

It was appropriate that the ticket windows for long-distance travel be located in this baronial setting. Long-distance travel was defined as anything west of Albany or south of New York City, and arranging for it was a heady business. It required the consultation of massive and mysterious tomes, the writing of routes on elongated but narrow documents, and the meticulous stamping with rubber stamps on every unoccupied square inch. Then there followed involved fiscal calculations as the traveler shifted from foot to foot and viewed with apprehension the mounting size of the figures to the left of the decimal point. If Pullman travel was involved, the process was duplicated with other documents analogous in size and shape but different in color. Finally a price was reached and met, and the traveler was duly authorized to board his train, find the hard green seating surface to which his lower berth was reduced in daylight hours, and settle down to watch western Massachusetts or southern Connecticut roll by until the blessed hour had come when he could seek the diner and break the ride with the one feasible diversion the eastern roads then offered to those on board.

The first of the two railroads that the South Station served was the Boston and Albany, which used the first half dozen tracks or so on the right as one entered the station. The B&A was a feeder line thrown off by the New York Central a bit south of Albany. It wound its leisurely and bouncy way down through the Berkshire hills, served the complex of Connecticut River cities that cluster about Springfield, moved on to the heart of the Commonwealth at Worcester, and so reached Boston and the South Station. In and of itself it offered relatively little by way of vacation possibilities and never made a bid for vacation trade, except in the sense that it was Massachusetts' gateway to the west and everything that connoted. The New York Central could advertise the Golden West, and pay for the advertisements.

Indeed the New York Central could do more. It could pay the $9.00 annual dividend it contracted to pay on every share of Boston and Albany stock when in the fine flush of fin de siecle railroading it contracted to do so for ninety-nine years. It did so in good times, and more important it did so in bad. Then came the Depression and unprecedented deficits for the New York Central. The $9.00 dividend still came in to the great satisfaction of those who had bought a stock that flickered back and forth in the 90-110 range, trusting to the monumental integrity and Gibraltar-like soundness of the New York Central. Mention of these qualities may strike a discordant note to those with fiscal interests in that marriage of semi-compatible interests and quasi-financial convenience, the Penn Central. We speak of the certainties of a half century ago, not the dubieties of today. Boston was dwarfed by New York early in the eighteenth century, but the fiscal acumen of Boston was never dwarfed by the fiscal acumen of New York. The $9.00 dividend financial wizards of New York had to pay all through the Depression to old ladies who lived on Beacon Hill is eloquent on that point.

We are straying from our subject, the great American vacation, as memories of the B&A tempt one to do. To finish the modest tale of the line the queen of whose fleet was once the New England States and which now may have a Budd liner or two in operation at the moment of reading, one records that somehow a means was found to get the New York Central off the financial hook by exchanging B&A stock for high yield bonds, and then the B&A disappeared into the maw and ceased to be. Today freight trains wind their leisurely and bouncy way along its modest length. When we turn, however, to the other railroad which used the rest of the tracks of the South Station, we are securely back again upon our subject. It was and within its limitations still is the New Haven Railroad, as the New York, New Haven and Hartford Railroad is always known.

The New Haven was rich in vacation possibilities. One division of it, known as the Old Colony in memory of the days when the New Haven was not a system but a set of separate railroads, served southeastern Massachusetts and this is indeed vacation land. North of Boston, thanks as much to Robert Frost as anyone else, is a phrase fairly well known. South of Boston is an equally valid if less known geographic term. We have already cited Rachel Carson and her tripartite division of the Atlantic seaboard, with the rocky division ending at Boston and the sandy division taking over. This is an incipient fact at Boston, an accomplished fact at Plymouth. The area between is the South Shore, with rock and sand alternating and indeed with areas in which sand on occasion buries the rock and on the next occasion rock shakes off the sand as shifting winds and water currents ordain. Rocks probing their green and dripping fingers into surging

New York Public Library

Nineteenth-century vacationers at Newport, Rhode Island.

surf make for splendid scenery, but no swimming. Such scenery is available in God's plenty north of Boston, much less so south. An unusual example south of Boston lies off Jerusalem Road in Cohasset.

A sandy expanse never threatened by rocks may or may not make for splendid scenery according to taste, but it does make for swimming. The swimming is magnificent off the great sandbar that stretches from Green Harbor south until it forms the northern protection for Plymouth harbor. The real problem is presented by the stretch that is rock one season and sand the next, for reasons far beyond the ken of the vacationer and the powers of the Chamber of Commerce to amend. It provides the sort of uncertainty that makes unlikely major investment in summer property by the prosperous, but also makes possible more modest investment by those whose means make the taking of some chances inevitable if they are to own summer homes. This fact has dictated much of the social pattern of the Massachusetts South Shore. The other fact that has dictated in stentorian tones is the temperature of the water. The Atlantic Ocean certainly, and very likely the other oceans as well, is a maze of massive and intricately interwoven rivers. One great river flows up the eastern seaboard, coming close enough to the south side of Cape Cod to affect its water temperature. This is a warm river and is called the Gulf Stream. Another great river flows down the eastern seaboard and keeps enough of its momentum to affect the water temperature of the South Shore. This is a cold river and is called the Labrador Current. In the summer there can be a twenty-degree difference in temperature between the water south of Cape Cod and the water north of the Cape and along the South Shore. For the inexperienced in such matters, one might say that water at 75° Fahrenheit as it frequently is in the summer months on the south side of the Cape makes for mild and pleasant swimming, shock-proof where the system is concerned. Water at 55° Fahrenheit as it frequently is in summer months on the South Shore causes the toes to freeze and threaten to drop off the feet. On the other hand, even South Shore water is balmy compared to the brew the frost demons concoct for the North Shore and the coast of Maine, whereas along the far northern strands of Prince Edward Island what is known in Massachusetts as "Cape water" reappears, a major blessing for Canadians who by and large are an underprivileged people where tolerable temperatures are concerned. Oceanography is for the specialists, but anyone can test its components and even without specialized knowledge may surmise what their effect is on coast property.

Fifty years ago there were two towns on the South Shore of Massachusetts that were prototypes of summer beach colonies along the North Atlantic seaboard. They were Scituate and Marshfield. Cohasset to the north has a stern and rock-bound coast, a few yards back from which the wealthy built their pleasure domes. It was an accepted principle of the period that the permanent rock coast was for the aristocracy, and aristocratic settlements grew at such places as Cohasset in Massachusetts, Rye in New Hampshire and Bar Harbor in Maine. South of Marshfield was Duxbury, with a land-locked yacht harbor and a tradition of undiluted Yankeedom that went back to those early and respected residents, John and Priscilla Alden. Beyond Duxbury was Plymouth, a historic shrine on a shallow harbor with a faint suggestion of the urban to its main street. South of Plymouth, however, were summer outcroppings of the Scituate-Marshfield sort. What made these communities prototypes was that their counterparts punctuated the Maine coast south of Portland, edged into New Hampshire's narrow corridor to the sea, were not unknown on the basically aristocratic North Shore, burgeoned forth triumphantly in Rhode Island, were to be found in Connecticut, had a field day in New Jersey, and had their southern equivalents wherever surf met sand east of the steaming cities of the hinterland.

The Old Colony Railroad served these summer settlements well, with several stations in both Scituate and Marshfield on a line that conscientiously followed the contours of the South Shore as far as Plymouth. Trains ran to and from Boston at hours consistent with the working patterns in the city, and intermittently in the midday. It was quite possible for a

family man to station his family in either town for the
summer, to be with them night and morning, to read his
morning *Globe* on the way up to the city and his evening
Traveler on the way down, to get in a swim before supper
and in a few semi-fabulous cases before breakfast (either
toes were welded on more firmly then or 55° was warmer
than it is now), to catch a whiff of vacation all summer and
to saturate himself in its delights during his two weeks off.

Both communities were simple, whether one's viewpoint is
architectural, sociological or economic. There were no houses
at the beach, only cottages. (We intercalate a footnote for
New Yorkers, New Jerseyites and any others who incline to
mid-Atlantic nomenclature. In Massachusetts the entire
seashore community is called the beach, provided it is
fringed with sand.) A cottage was a small dwelling encased
in a porch. A tolerable porch guarded two sides of the
cottage, a respectable porch three sides, and a good porch ran
all around the house. There were rocking chairs on the porch,
with seats and backs plaited with strips made from the
bamboo or some close relative. Inside on the first floor were
the living room, the dining room and the kitchen. The walls
of the rooms were the inside of the planks that comprised the
outside walls of the house. The inside walls were punctuated
by vertical joists to which might be pinned calendars, tables
of the tides, Old Colony timetables and similar objets d'art.
Living room furniture was pre-Grand Rapids and inclined
toward one of two extremes, a Spartan hardness in the seat
or a Corinthian voluptuousness of padding, marred by slits
out of which bulged some whitish-gray stuffing with what
looked like caraway seeds in it. There was invariably a
dining room, with a table of oak that had served the family
well in the city before the fashion for veneer took over, with
chairs and sideboard to match.

In the kitchen, along with the array of pots and pans and
the storage shelves for dishes concealed behind curtains of
flowered chintz or possibly curtains embellished with the
picture of the bowsprit of some long since foundered craft,
was the coal stove. It was so called, but it was a misnomer in
Scituate and Marshfield. There was no coal in either, but

there was pine wood cut in convenient lengths and sold at a stiff price by local woodsmen. To start the fire, one crumpled last night's *Traveler*, cradled wood on it, primed it with a good spurt from the kerosene can, and tossed in a lighted match. The culinary results were every bit as good as anything cooked by computer in this electronic age.

Up the uncarpeted stairs were two bedrooms, separated by a partition that rose six or seven feet above the floor but left ample space beneath the peaked roof for the fore and aft flow of air from the front and back windows. The woodshed was outside the house, adjoining the outhouse and with it constituting a modest duplex ancillary to the main establishment. The space between adjacent cottages ranged from an aperture just wide enough for a small child to get caught up to a capacious six feet. There was only so much beach and all the cottages possible had to be squeezed in beside it, and the sort of thinking basic to zoning laws was entertained by no one of sound mind.

Scituate and Marshfield were by no means identical. Scituate had a rising and falling coastline. Four times Scituate soared, modestly to be sure, and as it soared to its four cliffs which were edged with rock the elegance of the beach property that crowned these eminences rose with them. Four times the earth dipped to meet the water, and there was sand and so behind it cottages of the sort we have described. Marshfield had neither the lofty heights nor the water level depths of Scituate. Its shoreline gradually rose to a bluff which maintained a fairly steady height until it rose at its southern end to a genuine headland, once the site of a very early radio station and later the abode of mobile homes for summer residents.

One recalls the rumor that got around about that radio station, that from its soaring metallic mast the magicians in the shack below could talk to the Coast Guard boat at sea, not talk so to speak in the relatively familiar dot and dash but actually talk with the human voice. Sensible people dismissed the rumor, since no one had actually heard what one imagined would certainly have been a stentorian voice, to be heard far out at sea. It was not long after that we ourselves were tinkering with crystal sets that brought in a whisper from Amrad, the Voice of the Air at Medford Hillside, Massachusetts, while the affluent had sets run by electricity, with tubes in them and earphones that could be put in a soup bowl and everyone crowded about could hear. From that it was a simple step to the megaphone with ears at the bottom to which the earphones could be attached and all hear quite clearly without crowding. Once science had achieved that megaphone, it was a courteous gesture to invite folks to hear the afternoon concert from two to four, or the evening concert from eight to ten. The talent was amateur but its willingness was unbounded. It was a magnificent tribute to be invited to sing or play over Amrad, the Voice of the Air, and no artist would dream of declining. Whether Amrad helped the cause of religion in a profound sense is open to doubt, but it certainly helped to keep up numbers in the church choirs.

There was in a retrospect that we are confident has about it a good measure of reality a very wholesome and today enviable simplicity to summer life in Scituate and Marshfield, and in all the Scituates and Marshfields that began just south of Portland and ended just east of New Orleans, if indeed they ended there. Our specific Scituate and Marshfield served a double vacation purpose, as an objective for the last two weeks in July but also as a summer home for families with commuting fathers. We rather imagine that the latter role was somewhat more common than the former, and very much more common then than now.

Too little has been said in defense of the commuters' train, and a great deal can be said. It was not particularly fast nor particularly comfortable, but it was faster than a private car on a crowded highway into the city is today and it was very much more comfortable. It had a single destination, to be sure, but so did the commuters. They worked in downtown Boston. It was somewhat more practical from Scituate than from Marshfield, partly because Scituate was nearer to Boston and partly because the Scituate stations were nearer to the beach than those of Marshfield. Except for the grandfathers of today's joggers who made the station on foot, commuting fathers had to be driven to the station by their wives if there was in the family that relative rarity, an automobile, or they had to make their way by the public transportation available in the summer months. In this connection public transportation is a grandiose term although an exact one. In Marshfield an entrepreneur operated several large and lumbering buses with open sides and seats across the entire width of the vehicle. They were modelled, it may be, on the open streetcar of the era and they were known locally as barges. The barge doggedly plowed its way along while small boys gaily outdistanced it on their bicycles, waving happily at their parents and urging them to get a horse. The fathers could travel in a horse-drawn coach on Saturday, when business was especially brisk. The horse-drawn vehicle was jerkier than the barge but faster, although with an open road and a tail wind the barge could make the four miles to the Marshfield station in twenty minutes.

Once father was safely off and the breakfast dishes washed, it was time for the beach. The concept of the private beach was unknown in Scituate and Marshfield, either because the towns had acquired their beaches as town parks or because the concept of the private beach was like the concept of zoning, an idea whose hour for spontaneous generation had not yet dawned. It would have been a self-defeating idea in any case, since Marshfield especially was a battleground between rock and sand, and the tide of battle ebbed and flowed not merely from year to year but sometimes from month to month. The rocks were always there. The only question was, will they be covered this summer by sand or not? Some summers certain stretches of beach were sandy that other summers were rocky wastelands. There was one blessed part of Marshfield called Green Harbor that was always sandy. It was the tremendous sandbar already mentioned which in its lower reaches gave Duxbury its sheltered yacht basin and went on to be the northern bulwark of Plymouth harbor. Green Harbor was enviable in this regard, but aficionados of the Marshfield beaches to the north pointed out that Green Harbor had neither elevated bluffs nor a casino. These abodes of the blessed, Ocean Bluff and Brant Rock, had both. We shall return to the casino when time permits.

A private beach would have been a delusion and a snare, since what would be a magnificent stretch of soft white sand when purchased could easily be a seaweed-festooned, crab-infested wilderness of slimy rock the following June. The point fortunately was academic. The beach was for all in all parts, and one merely went where the sand was and gave the matter no further thought. What required much deeper thought was the matter of entering the water. There were some mothers to whom such a thought would have been unimaginably terrifying had some contrary impulse put it in their heads. They were dressed for bathing. That is to say, they had put on the somber black outfit that then connoted bathing. There was the elongated black blouse that continued earthward until it ceased to be blouse and was true skirt, concealing except when the wind freshened the voluminous black bloomers worn beneath. Mother had drawn on the long black stockings she wore for bathing, and laced her black bathing shoes. She had firmly on her head the white bathing hat with the moderately undulating brim which gave the one touch of color to the otherwise funereal outfit appropriate to the pleasant pastime of bathing. The bathing outfits women wore, with their billowing blouses and ballooning bloomers, were not entirely different from the costumes worn by the Seljuk Turks when they emerged from Turkestan in the eleventh century.

Sheer prudence dictated that at the liberal uttermost they be considered bathing costumes. Swimming in one would be foolhardy, inviting the fate of Ophelia of whom the Queen said:

Her clothes spread wide;
And, mermaid-like, awhile they bore her up:
Which time she chanted snatches of old tunes. . . .

There was nothing in the pattern of matronly thought in the 1920s to suggest that a woman would float helplessly, singing tunes from *No, No, Nanette*, "Till that her garments, heavy with their drink, Pull'd the poor wretch from her melodious lay To muddy death." Consequently bathing was accomplished in shallow water, and comprised a few shivering splashes and some breathtaking dunks.

A water nymph named Annette Kellerman liberated women of the Roaring Twenties from natatorial surplusage when she introduced a daring device called the one-piece suit, a form-fitting affair that reached from a trifle below the neck to a trifle above the knee but did permit a woman to swim once she learned how. Here the matter may rest. Assuming that womanly attractiveness of features and form is a constant in all generations, whether the bathing outfit of the 1920s which left everything to the imagination or the bikini of the 1970s which leaves nothing should be deemed the more seductive is a question for philosophy. Children of both sexes wore one-piece suits and swam, while their mothers watched, talked, knitted and, when they went out too far, prayed.

The beach and the porch gave rest and relaxation by day, with an occasional foray to pick blueberries or to visit. The Casino gave entertainment and activity by night. At this point some rigorous defining is in order. One must prune from the subconscious any image of Monte Carlo or Las Vegas. The Marshfield casinos were not of that stamp. There were two, one in Brant Rock and one in Ocean Bluff. There was none in Green Harbor and, unless memory has slipped a cog, none in Scituate. The two Marshfield casinos were similar, with the one in Ocean Bluff a shade the more elegant of the two. It had four parts. The first was an ice-cream parlor. It was obligatory in the period that an ice-cream parlor contain marble-topped tables of miniscule surface area, and that one sit on a chair with an inadequate sitting surface and a back of convoluted iron tubing tastefully colored and embellished with metallic rosettes. All the physical discomfort, however, was external. The sundaes, known locally as college ices, were lavishly adorned with ultra-sweet pineapple syrup or super-rich chocolate sauce, and the latter had the added glory of walnut segments substantial in both size and number. To say that we have

such sundaes today is like saying that we have our play-
wrights today just as the Elizabethans had their recently
quoted Shakespeare. And yet this may well be the sort of
chauvinism rooted in time rather than place. Few things in
life are so nearly changeless as ice-cream recipes and penny
candy. The writer recently stood before a counter of penny
candy in Minnesota. There was not a type of candy in the

A bathing casino.   *New York Public Library*

counter that had not been perfectly familiar to him sixty
years ago in Massachusetts. Time and place had changed
nothing, and he counted this a major blessing for juvenile St.
Paul.

The second part of the Casino was the poolroom, known by
official nomenclature as the billiards room. For some reason
sunk deep in the collective Massachusetts subconscious was
the conviction that pool was a disreputable affair whereas
billiards was a gentleman's game. The point was academic

where the Casino was concerned, its moral tone being uniformly exemplary in all its parts. Indeed to say that it was as elevated in tone as the church would be unfair to the Casino, considering what has gone on in recent years in many churches. Management provided cushion segments to fit over the pockets and thus change a pool table into a billiards table, but they were in little demand. Billiards was little in demand at the Casino, possibly because the social milieu of Ocean Bluff was not one to which billiards was native, possibly also because billiards is too difficult a game for the sort of person who patronized the Casino between the Fourth of July and Labor Day, to whom a game of pool was a rare summer diversion and not a year-around preoccupation or an outlet for the gambling instinct. Mothers kept a close eye on the poolroom, however, fearing contagion even in so morally sterilized an atmosphere as that of the Casino.

Bowling was a game for one and all. A bowling alley was never considered disreputable, even when it was, and in the hilarity that engulfed the Casino bowling alleys, lack of skill was on the whole more highly esteemed than skill itself. Furthermore, bowling was for both sexes, whereas no lady ever entered a billiards room. A sharp distinction must be drawn, however, between the atmosphere that prevailed normally and the tension that rose when the men's bowling league met, the ladies' bowling league met, or both leagues met in a battle of the sexes. When a strike is worth a quarter and a spare a dime, and even a ten has some point value, levity is not the spirit to let reign, and the league matches were for blood as well as money. Most of the time, however, the alleys were patronized by the hilariously inept, the most gifted of whom were capable of hitting themselves on the ankle with the ball or bouncing it into the next alley. Always bearing in mind that Massachusetts still is only affiliated with the rest of the union, as the 1972 elections showed, one should be aware that in Massachusetts one bowls at candlepins, elongated and slender pins which taper at both ends, not tenpins. To average 95 at candlepins indicates skill of a high order.

The first three parts of the Casino were located on the first floor. The fourth part was upstairs, but what it was differed with the hour of the day and even the day of the week. On rare occasions by daylight hours it was a meeting hall. Six nights a week it was a moving-picture theatre, and on Tuesday, Thursday and Saturday nights a dance hall as well. Since six nights of dancing a week was a high and prime requisite of the era, the Brant Rock Casino dovetailed its schedule with that of Ocean Bluff, offering dancing on Monday, Wednesday and Friday. When it was a moving-picture theatre massive tarpaulins covered the floor and movable chairs linked in units of four provided the seats. When the show was over, these could be stacked in quick order, the tarpaulins rolled, the moving-picture screen furled, the orchestra seated on the miniscule stage and on with the dance. The reconstituting of the seating arrangement was a leisurely morning task for the management and crew except on Saturday night, when emergency measures were necessary to set up the seats again. On Sunday morning it was a Catholic church.

The movies of the era have never entirely passed out of the national awareness, since there is a temperament for which the past has the attraction that the future has for a different temperament. But what is remembered is the highlight, not the habitual dim glow. What is largely forgotten is the newsreel that opened the show, a pictorial presentation by Pathé of some photogenic event of the not too distant past about which one had read in the daily paper. Then there was the comedy, a very short bit of slapstick performed in the very attenuated tradition of Charlie Chaplin. A Charlie Chaplin picture was much too important to be a comedy in that sense. It was a feature, and in the best of them pathos had a way of taking over from comedy and elevating it. One recalls Buster Keaton, Fatty Arbuckle and Harold Lloyd as having sufficient talent to rise above the ruck and be theatrical figures in their own right, and one recalls the Keystone Cops as the embodiment of slapstick at its limited best. As a rule there was one feature picture a night at the Casino, since the decks had to be cleared for dancing by ten, and in the serene judgment of the Casino management one feature picture was enough. There were limits to the extent twenty-five cents might be expected to go, even fifty years ago.

Management knew its patronage with crystal clarity and accepted only feature pictures guaranteed to meet the widest common denominator of family approval. As a matter of fact, there was little else available anyway. On one occasion the Casino did show Theda Bara in *The Vamp*, but that was a daring deviation from the norm. One should add that there was a new feature every night of the week and every week of the summer. Not only could one go to the movies every night, but many did. A recollection that may well be blurred and astigmatic suggests that all features were variants on themes by Mary Pickford or Douglas Fairbanks, and if one allows heresy to be added to astigmatism one would even contend that all heroines looked like Mary Pickford and acted as much like her as their talents allowed, just as all the heroes with the exception of William S. Hart were not only of the tribe of Douglas Fairbanks but related to him by blood as well. On the other hand, if the central characters did not seem to change, it was a different picture and therefore in a limited sense a different story each night.

Competition was strenuous among the youthful frequenters of the Casino to see the show from the best imaginable vantage point, inside the projection booth itself. The pictures were shown through a projection machine operated by a handle, and it was a wearying matter literally to grind out a newsreel, a comedy and a feature picture. The operator was more than willing to be relieved by a juvenile sufficiently enthralled by the grandeur of it all to obey implicitly the instructions not to grind too quickly to speed up the chases on horseback nor too slowly to prolong the kissing scenes. Always one had to be prepared to drop before the lens either the card which read *End of the Reel* or the one which read *Please Excuse Us for a Minute*. The latter was used when the film broke and had to be spliced.

Three nights a week there was dancing at the Casino. This was the heyday of body-to-body dancing, with the foxtrot and the waltz predominating. Square dancing had been relegated to that subdivision of the past deemed comic, and the farthest sighted could not foresee its revival. The individualized dance in which man faced woman as both went through contortions was still veiled by the kindness of an unimagined future. The dance has always ranked a respectable fourth to wine, woman and song among the perils of the human race, but it was not clear to the writer then nor is it clarified now why that anticipation of the later vogue in dancing, the Charleston, which depended on the unnatural inward twisting of the knees and a vague flapping of the arms, was considered the dance appropriate to those making their terpsichorean way down the primrose path. If any dance was seductive, it would seem to have been the waltz, with its dreamy cadences, its cheek-to-cheek posture, its thigh-to-thigh glide. On the contrary, no dance was more highly esteemed by competent moralists than the waltz and the contrary thesis, that the more muscular agility a dance required the more daring it was, and consequently the more seductive, was universally held. The truth was that seduction, although probably not totally absent from Ocean Bluff life, was never a major problem and so its methods and dimensions stayed in the happy realm of the academic.

The deeper truth was that a basic decency pervaded life in Ocean Bluff and Brant Rock, in Scituate and Marshfield, and in all the Scituates and Marshfields that lined the American seaboard from Maine to Florida, from British Columbia to Southern California, and wherever inland places of their sort developed. They rested on the firm foundation that the unit of life is not the individual but the family. Summer homes were possible in them for persons of modest means because summer homes themselves were modest. There was nothing about them to suggest the vacationing aristocrat, not even in the summer hotels present in them. The supposition that on summer vacation life is stripped down to the essentials pervaded the hotels quite as truly as the cottages, and one neither expected nor got in them the luxuries and refinements of city hotels. Neither did one get at the end of two weeks a bill beyond the modest means of the reasonably successful wage earner. In such summer colonies one did not live the life of the vacationing Indian, although the Indian's spirit was closer than that of the aristocrat. Indians exemplified Thoreau's thesis that the other way to grow richer is to cut down your wants, and the less you wanted at a summer home the better able you were to afford one.

Vacation centered about a few fundamentals: a sweep of ocean, an expanse of sand, the steady stirring of cool air where warm sand meets cool water; the play of children and the small talk of mothers watching them; the wait for father to arrive on the barge and the agreement that he was entitled to a short dip and the children to a bonus dip with him while mother manipulated cooking utensils on the wood-burning stove to keep things from cooking too fast. There was the small talk on the porch at evening with the husband and wife across the way, and for young people the walk on the darkened beach and the talk not quite so small that went with it. There were the varied delights of the Casino: the walk up followed by the college ice, the game of kelly pool, the impromptu and frantic bowling match by three inept husbands and their suddenly angular and disjointed wives, the picture with Mary Miles Minter in it and the dance to "Beautiful Ohio," "Little Nellie Kelly" tunes, and "Peggie O'Neil." On the horizon was Labor Day, but the horizon was far away and only in the moment of morbidity that childhood knows when the thought of school again crosses the mind did the distant horizon cross one's mental line of sight.

Labor Day always came. The days before were ominous with preparation, as trunks were loaded for the hour when the express truck would come to carry them to the station where they would be checked on one's railroad ticket and carried back to Boston. Beyond was the final hour when the water would be turned off and the traps drained, and in some cottages the wooden skirts that in summer concealed the piles on which they rested pulled up so the rampaging tides of winter could surge beneath and do no damage. To lock up the cottage was a matter of no great moment. What was there in it to steal, and who was there to do the stealing? And so the day of departure came, the barges shuttled back and forth to the station, farewells echoed across the fields and streets, there was the frantic race out to the beach for one last look at the ocean while parents tapped impatient feet, and in the night a silence rested over Ocean Bluff.

Here and there was a lighted cottage, where some retired couple stayed to enjoy solitude and peace until there was a hint of frost and they would take the hint. The post office was still open and would be all winter long, and so would the store in which it was located. Here and there, for reasons obscure then and obscure now, people of severely limited means stayed in cottages that had been winterized by the crude and ineffective methods of the day, where living rooms were made stifling by wood fires in cast-iron stoves and bedrooms above made livable to those inured to cold by eddies of warmth that occasionally penetrated registers in the ceilings above the stoves. Probably they stayed because they had no place to go, but they were few in number and one imagines that for them the winter was indeed their winter of discontent. It was of the essence of Ocean Bluff that it was a place for one season only, and that a sign reading "Closed for the Season" could quite appropriately be hung above the road leading to it from the railroad station.

For two summer months it was a place of delight, for four winter months a place of desolation, for the autumn months a place of happy memory and for the spring months a place of hopeful promise. Those happy few who owned automobiles would drive down for a last look in autumn and for as many first looks as possible in spring. Now and then a sunny, snowfree Sunday invited a mid-winter look, but not every off-season visitor opened his cottage on such occasions. It was indeed "Closed for the Season."

It was typical of all the Ocean Bluffs and Brant Rocks of the period that they were summer appendages to full-time American towns. There was behind Ocean Bluff a Marshfield where people lived the year around, and behind the summer Scituate was the year around Scituate. There was an amazing degree of separation between the summer colony and the permanent town. Except for the townspeople who did business with the summer visitors there was no communication between them, nor did anyone consider this strange. Prices at the store were hiked up a notch the first of July, dropped back a notch after Labor Day, but few objected since the notch was not too far up the economic yardstick and there was summer help to be paid. Since the summer colony needed no public services ten months of the year and at all times got the barest modicum of fire protection and other services, the taxes it paid came extraordinarily close to sheer profit for the town and it was mainly for this reason that the colony was deemed a town asset. Otherwise the townies were as oblivious of the summer people as the latter were of the townies. The summer people were of the city and the natives were of the town, and never the twain did meet.

7. *One day if by land, two if by sea*

 One of the major losses suffered by Boston in the past half century we have already mentioned, the loss of the Atlantic Ocean. The physical ocean is still there, serving as a receptacle for the Charles and Mystic Rivers and providing a highway for the sugar ships and "banana wagons" that still unload at the Hub. What is all but totally gone is the Atlantic Ocean as a highway to adventure and romance, one of the great arteries of vacation travel. There is still a boat to Nantasket and a boat to Provincetown, precious to be sure but vestigial remains of what once was. There is not even a ferry to East Boston.

There was a time when Boston had a ship to almost anywhere on the seven seas. This is not a rhetorical flourish, since it was a port of call for the Dollar Line with ships that called each month on a route that brought them around the world. Cunard and North German Lloyd used it regularly to northern European ports, and sailings to the Mediterranean were frequent. Our present scale of literary operations, however, is too modest to admit consideration of anything like the Grand Tour, and in the days of which we speak any trip to Europe bore a more than passing resemblance to a Grand Tour. Let us limit our memories to coastal voyages.

There was the Eastern Steamship boat to New York. This left after the working day was over, coasted down the South Shore in the evening twilight, had people clinging to the rails as it threaded its way through the Cape Cod Canal, and then moved into the darkness of Buzzards Bay and the waters of

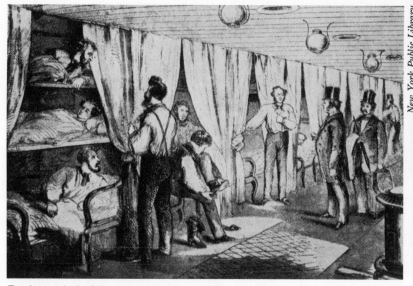

Peripatetic bedchamber: A nineteenth-century sleeping car.

Long Island Sound beyond. It emerged again into the daylight as it came up New York Harbor, with the topless towers of Manhattan rising from the haze and slipping again into the mist, with tugboats scurrying hither and yon like smoking water beetles, and some mastodon of a freight train implausibly floating across the harbor from New Jersey. There are two superbly fine ways to get a first view of New York, to come up the harbor early in the morning and to cross the Hell Gate Bridge by train in the perfect clarity of an autumn sunset. You got the first from the New York boat. What is more, if just a shade of casuistry is permitted, it used to be the second quickest way of getting to New York on business. The quickest way was the midnight train, The Owl, which pulled out of the South Station at midnight and drifted quietly and effortlessly down to New York, stopping nowhere en route and taking longer to get there than any other train between the cities but always conscious that there were people on board asleep. The Owl and the boat both put you in the city at the start of a working day, something no train leaving in the morning could do and no plane now flying in the morning can do. For competition the Boston-New York boat had, in addition to The Owl, the Fall River boat. One took the train to Fall River, boarded the ship, and thereafter one's experience was like the one offered by the rival ship, minus the Cape Cod Canal. As testimony to the thesis that one lives longer in a nation's songs than in its laws, the Old Fall River Line still lives in tuneful melody but the Eastern Steamship boat rests in undisturbed peace. Which was the better way to go to New York occasioned fierce debate, and the ashes of that debate need no stirring.

Then there were the Merchant and Miner ships for ports more distant. They swung out to sea, rounded Cape Cod at Provincetown, stood well off shore until the point of landfall was approached, and then they made their choices. One headed around Cape May and up the Delaware to Philadelphia and another rounded Cape Charles, headed in to Norfolk and then steamed up the long and sinuous reaches to Baltimore. No slower way of reaching Baltimore save walking existed, but if anyone ever contested that the train ride across the featureless New Jersey steppes and the Delaware-Maryland littoral was a better buy than the ride up Chesapeake Bay his name is mute and inglorious in the annals. Then there were the vessels that clove the sea path far enough to warrant talk not of boat rides but of voyages. There was the boat to Savannah and to Jacksonville. This service existed thanks to the geographic quirk that makes the Atlantic coast shelve in toward the west and the Pacific coast toward the east, so that Jacksonville is about as far west as Cleveland and the distance by land from Jacksonville to Los Angeles hundreds of miles shorter than from Boston. These miles were translated into substantial savings where slow moving freight was concerned, since to ship by train is considerably more expensive than to ship by boat. The Savannah boat was a slow way to the South, but not much slower than the drive today. The finest of all these southern voyages, however, was the Morgan Line route from Boston to New Orleans, a route which gave you an Atlantic voyage, a view of the Florida coast which already was beginning to burgeon forth with places of refuge from winter, a swing around the Keys, a leisurely arc through the Gulf and then the ride up the Mississippi along that thread of river which winds its way through a landscape not entirely land and certainly not sea but somehow an amalgam of two elements, until the city is reached and the glories of New Orleans unfold.

All these ships are one with Nineveh and Tyre, and yet something remains from them that should not be discounted. The ship as a means of transportation for passengers has largely vanished. It is now just barely possible for a vacationer to cross the Atlantic by boat. As for present-day ocean travel south from Boston, one may choose between Nantasket and Provincetown, but naturally only in the summer. And yet, the passenger ship has survived. It is no longer of vital consequence where it goes, and indeed the "Cruise to Nowhere" is a popular Boston venture. There are cruises about the Caribbean, or shorter junkets to Bermuda. There are ventures into the delightfully illogical, like the Bermuda-Halifax-Saguenay triangle. There are more elaborate excursions to sea by the Mediterranean, or to North Cape, or to South America, or around the world. All this attests to a fundamental fact: the ship is the one means of transportation enjoyable and enjoyed for its own sake, and strong enough in its attraction to make the cruise ship profitable despite its massive operating costs. Some people like to fly, but the writer has yet to hear of the first "Flight to Nowhere." There are those who like train travel, but the pleasure ride for railroad buffs has a small if select company. Even the pleasure ride in the family car undertaken without destination is a dwindling venture, and if there are those who seek bus travel for its own sweet sake their number is closer to corporal's guard than to legion. But the ship is different. On the ship the ride is the thing, with all the appurtenances that can go with the ride on a ship but on no other vehicle.

By the popularity of the cruise ship today one should measure the lure of the coastal service along the Atlantic seaboard in the 1920s. But one cannot measure its endless variety, one aspect of which was the financial, by anything the cruise can offer. Unless memory is badly off, a five-dollar bill brought you to New York and the charge to ports beyond was commensurate. A stateroom was inexpensive and the cost of the dinner broke no backs. You could sail from Boston to New York every night, to Europe just about every week and around the world at least once a month. Perhaps New York and Philadelphia were one day if by land, two if by sea, but one day was a business trip whereas two days were a vacation. The popularity of the current cruise ship proves the point.

Hitherto our consideration has been limited to ships that sailed south of Boston, with passing reference to those that sailed east. As a matter of practical fact, where vacation was concerned the boats that sailed north were of even greater importance. One could reach Maine or Down East in one day by land, but the better way was the leisurely way, two days by sea. It was better even when the first day was only the stub of a day, starting after the business offices closed.

It was a quite short stub where Portland, Maine, was concerned, and it did take a fairly firm dedication to sea travel to choose the night afloat to Portland over the shade more than two hours it took on the best of the Boston & Maine trains. Nevertheless generation after generation turned out those adequately dedicated. It was possible to go by ship from Boston to Portland as early as 1824, when the *Patent*, "strong, commodious and elegantly fitted for passengers," started the Boston-Portland run. By 1845 there was a Bangor boat from Boston. Service expanded and became competitive, and when service becomes sufficiently competitive it tends to become self-destructive. The formation of the already mentioned Eastern Steamship Lines through the combination of what had been six separate lines averted self-destruction and Eastern Steamship thereafter provided overnight service to Maine until it succumbed to the automobile, the truck and the Depression.

Fifty years ago there was passenger service between Boston and Portland, Bath, Bangor and Eastport, the latter a stop on the line to St. John, New Brunswick. Except possibly in the case of Portland, the boat ride down was merely the prelude to adventure. Portland was an end in itself, although the vacationist with a destination at Peak's Island or Chebeague in Casco Bay had a pleasant sail before him. The Bath boat, on the other hand, was a prelude to genuine adventure as one boarded at Bath a minor-league Eastern Steamship to thread one's way through a maze of islands to such romantic outposts as Southport, Five Islands, Squirrel Island, Christmas Cove and ultimately Boothbay Harbor. Presumably these outposts ceased to exist after Labor Day, or one reached them from the railroad station at Wiscasset in some devious and painful fashion involving dirt roads, since the Bath boat never survived Labor Day by long and half a century ago the pavement in Maine stopped at Brunswick. The Bangor boat seems to a memory not impossibly bedimmed by time's sealing touch to have been the queen of the fleet. At least it clove the sea lanes of

An ornate chamber: The cabin of the ferryboat "Bergen," 1889.

New York Public Library

romance, burrowing through the eternal fog and making its landfall at Rockland at some implausible hour of the early morning and then moving up through the golden mists to Camden, Belfast, Winterport, the very name of which bespeaks the Penobscot in January, on to Bangor and a great, wide world beyond, much of it wilderness.

The Eastport boat was a bit of New England chauvinism. It was not the Eastport boat at all, but the St. John boat, but it did stop at Eastport and there one is Down East with a vengeance. Beyond lie those islands that are Canadian by ownership and American by geography, Campobello Island and Deer Island, and out where the fog is dense, the massive bulk of Grand Manan Island. There is something inexpressibly Down East about Passamaquoddy Bay, its deep and sinuous inlets, its islands and its ferries that cut their maze of furrows across its waters, each furrow different from the rest, each ferry knowing its own mission and performing it with single-minded devotion.

There was never a better destination than the State of Maine. We return once more to Rachel Carson and her tripartite division of the Atlantic seaboard: sand begins to take over from rock at Old Orchard Beach, Maine, but rock does not lose out to sand until one passes Boston and reaches Plymouth, Massachusetts. There are four fine beaches in Maine south of Old Orchard, at Kennebunk, Wells, Ogunquit and York. There are also fine rocky headlands like Cape Arundel at Kennebunkport, Bald Head Cliff at Ogunquit and the Nubble at York. North of Old Orchard what beaches there are tend to be small, usually the bottoms of coves rather than strands along the sea, and very often shingle instead of sand. Everywhere the water is perishingly cold, incredibly and intolerably cold. Nowhere in all America is water so cold as on the coast of Maine, not even in Lake Superior itself which is another watery abode of frost demons. And yet people swim, or at least bathe, or if one is picayune about truth, at any rate, dunk at Sand Beach on Mount Desert Island. Of such stuff are Indians made, when on vacation in Maine.

Let us start with the coast, contrasting the only true

vacation area of New Jersey with an important vacation area of Maine. The New Jersey coast is a strand, punctuated by inlets, estuaries, harbors and back waters, but dominated by sand. The Maine coast is a drowned coast, forced beneath the water by the ice cap of the last glacial age, which slowly shook off the icy water as the ice cap retreated and rose as best it could above the sea level. As it rose some rocky spines and massive headlands reestablished contact with the mainland. Water filled the valleys between and wound up through every interstice and crevice between the ridges to produce arteries and veins of water far inland from the ocean, but pulsing as the ocean pulses with every flood and ebb tide. Other rocky spines and massive headlands did not quite make it. They comprise the thousand or so islands off the Maine coast, some of them large enough to harbor voting precincts that regularly go Republican and others scraps of barren, seaweed festooned rock. It is 225 miles from Eastport to Kittery as the crow flies, 278 miles as the motorist drives on U.S. 1 and the Maine Turnpike, but twenty-five hundred miles if one follows every turn and twist of those rocky spines, massive headlands, watery valleys, veins and arteries of Nature that make up the coast of Maine.

A long, straight, sandy beach invited the de luxe approach to Nature in the days when only those whose means permitted the de luxe approach had vacations. Therefore it was the approach taken first at Long Branch and Cape May in New Jersey. The pattern was established at these two havens of contentment, and then adopted, enthusiastically expanded, imaginatively embellished and splendidly popularized at Atlantic City. Atlantic City was the pattern for the rest. No matter how democratized the Jersey shore was to become, no matter how massive the throngs on the boardwalk and beach in the high noon of summer, no matter how diluted the aristocratic ideal of the watering place was to be, the original concept that Nature is first to be methodized and improved and then enjoyed on the Jersey shore was never entirely obliterated. But that concept never took root in Maine. As a matter of fact, it could not because Maine does not have the coast for it. To some extent it rooted at those

Maine beaches that resemble the Jersey beaches. One can see
the results even today: Old Orchard for the light-hearted,
shoe-box lunch set, Wells for the family cottage, Ogunquit
for the artist and aesthete and York for the substantial
industrialist as a place to leave his family. But these four
beaches are only geographically Down East, not Down East
in the psychological sense. We must come to grips with the
question barely touched upon before. Where is Down East?

Outside New England, Down East is New England. That,
of course, is absurd. Are Bridgeport, Connecticut, and
Stockbridge, Massachusetts, in their several ways and indeed
they are several, Down East? In New England Down East is
Maine and the Canadian maritime provinces. That may stand
as a reasonable geographic definition. But there is a kind of
implicit psychological meaning of Down East that eliminates
on the one hand industrial cities like Biddeford, Waterville,
Moncton and St. John but eliminates as well such vacation
haunts of lords and ladies as Bar Harbor used to be and York
Harbor, Kennebunkport, St. Andrews and Ingonish still are.
It is easier to illustrate the psychological Down East than it
is to define it or to bound it. Consider the stretch of coast
from Frenchman Bay to Passamaquoddy Bay where there is
little more than rocks and wreaths of seaweed, pounding
surf and endless fogs, where trees are gnarled, twisted,
stunted and something like tundra creeps down to where the
bare rock begins. That is Down East with a vengeance, and
yet a land where Andrew Wyeth can find beauty, and human
warmth, understanding and compassion. Or Down East can
be any of the multitudinous lakes of Maine, starting with
Sebago just above Portland and continuing to the last and
least seen wilderness pond on the Allagash Waterway. Down
East cannot be too much of the workaday world, nor too
much of the world of elegance, but there is ample room in
Maine between the two and even more in the Maritimes. We
are now at our starting point.

The start of the Maine vacation began at a place that to
many still epitomizes it, Poland Springs. In 1794 Jabez
Ricker of Alfred, Maine, bought land from the Sabbathday
Lake Shakers, a little religious colony that still exists at New

Gloucester, up U.S. 202 if one leaves the Maine Turnpike at the Gray exit. He built a home and began to rent rooms to wayfarers. His hospitality was warm and comprehensive, and those who made the weary journey from Portland to Augusta, or even to nearby Auburn and Lewiston, were glad enough to break it at Poland. It took only two years for the Ricker house to become the Mansion House at Poland Springs. Yet one is mistaken if he reads into Poland Springs the story of Saratoga Springs. The springs were there, but Jabez Ricker never dreamed that they flowed nectar. This was the discovery of his grandson, Hiram Jabez Ricker, who grew thirsty haying, drank of the springs and found that the water cured his chronic dyspepsia. He spread the word through Mansion House, and when the guests sampled the waters they found them good. The Rickers, alert as only State of Mainers are alert to commercial possibilities, realized that the springs by which through pure chance they had built the Mansion House might flow with liquid gold. Springs were flowing with it all over Europe and at many places in America. They were right. For over a century Poland Spring Water remained high in popularity, and along with the Mansion House and lordlier and later Poland Spring House has flourished and deserved to flourish. The vacation of the lord and lady has never been more satisfactory than upon Ricker Hill, with its view over hills and lakes and the other view into that dining room with its magnificent cuisine. But Poland Springs was never Down East, nor pretended to be.

Just as the coastal forest had to be penetrated by the railroad before the Jersey shore could be vacation land, so the railroad and the steamboat had to reach Maine. The river valleys of Maine helped the one, its ample harbors the other. The railroads of Maine started like the pieces of a jigsaw puzzle, not only seemingly unrelated but actually so until a pattern was imposed upon them. The first line was built in 1836 along the Penobscot from Old Town to Bangor. The second came into being in 1840, from the miniscule settlement of Whitneyville, some ten miles or so up the Machias River, to Machiasport. The pines grew tall near Whitneyville, and Machiasport is entitled to its name by reason of the ample reaches and deep waters of Machias Bay. The railroads of Maine were first built to bring lumber to the wharves; there was a rationale behind the jigsaw pieces. In 1842 the Portland, Saco and Portsmouth Railroad began to operate, providing rail service from Boston to Portland, although the Boston and Maine Railroad, heir to these simple beginnings, did not come into being until 1873. Other railroads were built in interior Maine, in the valleys of the Androscoggin, Kennebec and Penobscot Rivers and across the ridges between them, until by 1890 there were thirty-one railroads in the state.

It is a blessed circumstance that their history is not our duty, and we limit ourselves to the barest bones of Maine's rich, diversified and in some places colorful railroad history. In 1881 the Consolidated Maine Central Railroad was put together out of five lines that served the area from Portland to Bangor. Now one could ride on a single ticket across that much of Maine. In 1862 the New Brunswick Railroad had been built from St. Andrews, N.B., to Houlton, Maine. It was a modest venture, but it was destined to become part of the Canadian Pacific short-cut from Montreal to the Maritimes that cleaves its furrow through the western wilderness and is the one train that today carries passengers in Maine. Nor should a lover of pomposity pass over the European and North American Railway, a line which fell short of its name but did reach from Bangor to Vanceboro and now, as part of the Maine Central, gives access to New Brunswick and to the Canadian National as it majestically glides from Halifax to Montreal, always staying in Canada as befits a publicly-owned facility. Nor indeed should one omit the Bangor and Aroostook which in 1894 reached Houlton and a few years later Fort Kent; the Bangor and Aroostook, omen and prodigy among American railroads, a line capable of making money.

Once the body of Maine had the arteries and veins of the three railroads that were in effect a single system, the Boston and Maine, the Maine Central and the Bangor and Aroostook, and once the chief ports of Maine had the contacts by sea with Boston and America beyond, the Maine

Lightning Express Trains Leaving the Junction (Currier and Ives)

vacation was a practical possibility. But the Maine vacation defies definition and perplexes analysis. Maine has always been so many different things to very many people. To take the familiar and already stressed, Maine has been a vacation by the seashore, the vacation compounded of surf and sun, lazy hours on the sand, lounging as a member of the rocking-chair brigade at an old-fashioned summer hotel. Maine in these respects has been simpler than New Jersey, but not basically different. But most of coastal Maine is not a strand but a rockbound shore. Maine has had a message for the artist, in any art. Maine has summoned the painter, the writer, the musician, the actor, and communities in Maine for many years have given summer harborage to those who paint, write, compose and act. Maine has summoned the lover of the picturesque, the pleasantly old-fashioned, the nostalgic. There are communities in Maine that have invited the sort of beautification that money and good taste can give, and have received it.

But there is a totally different Maine, the Maine that is still the largest wilderness this side of the Rockies. There has been the fisherman's Maine, the hunter's Maine, the hiker's Maine, the camper's Maine. There has been the Maine beloved of the solitary, where one could get fifty miles from a paved road and a hundred miles from anything larger than a hamlet. That also has been Maine and vacation land, the Maine into which you now are quite as apt to be flown as you are to drive. There is a Maine deep in the wilderness that is quite as truly the Maine of the wealthy as was Bar Harbor when it was the Newport of the North.

Happily there has also been a salutary modification of this Maine. There has been a Maine of lakes, streams, woods and quiet solitude that anyone could reach by train and later by family car, where one could vacation in old clothes and enjoy old pleasures in the happy pretense of the pseudo-Indian. It is difficult if not impossible to find a common denominator except the political by which to define Old Orchard Beach, Lakewood, Mt. Desert Island, Moosehead Lake, Mt. Katahdin and the Allagash Waterway. The closest one can come is a certain psychological denominator, the desire to get away from it all, to avoid the milling crowd, to simplify life for a few short, precious days.

Maine's final masterpiece of ocean, mountain, rock and pine is Mt. Desert Island. Mt. Desert is an island only by the bare technicality of a channel that separates it from the mainland and the town of Trenton. In 1836 the channel was bridged and on September 4, 1844, Thomas Cole crossed the bridge. Art had discovered Mt. Desert Island. Thomas Cole is considered the founder of the Hudson River school of painting, which was a pictorial by-product of the Romantic Movement and marked by an enthusiastic eye for the picturesque. Mt. Desert Island is rich in subjects for such a school and Thomas Cole was an artist in words as well as pigments. He publicized the island, and the wealthy listened to him. The next fifty years found Mt. Desert Island growing not so much into a Newport of the North as an escape from Newport, or perhaps more kindly, as an alternative to Newport.

Even in its palmiest days, and they were truly palmy, Bar Harbor was a curious blend of simplicity and ostentation. The wealthy built palaces on the island and took walks to collect flowers and shells. They erected baronial castles on ample acreage, and then built little cabins deep in the woods behind the castles to which they could retire and think "green thoughts in a green shade."

Pollution, as we know, is a hydra-headed affair. No sooner was the Bar Harbor ice supply secure and the wells cleaned up than the automobiles appeared. Summer rusticators had come to Bar Harbor to escape the noise, speed and restlessness that the auto epitomized. The era being one of law and order, a law was passed banning autos from Mt. Desert Island. The summer visitors applauded the law and the natives grumbled at it, but the summer visitor was the native's livelihood and he accepted the bitter with the sweet. The law stuck until 1913, but by then the glue was dry and the statute came apart, as it was to do a few years later on Nantucket Island. John D. Rockefeller found the logical compromise, one that a John D. Rockefeller could afford. He built fifty miles of graded carriage roads, and today Mt.

Desert Island has two road systems that intertwine with overpasses and underpasses but never meet. One is for carriages, which may now be translated riding horses, and the other is for automobiles. The past and the present are tangent on Mt. Desert but one is not superimposed upon the other.

Two events of this century provide the framework within which the modern history of the island is contained. The first was the brilliant and farsighted decision formed by George Bucknam Dorr and President Charles Eliot of Harvard and carried out with the promptness and energy characteristic of both men. The woodcutters had moved onto the island, and the melancholy history of the forests of America was about to be repeated. To preserve the majestic woodlands of Mt. Desert the two men induced the wealthy of Bar Harbor to buy up thousands of acres. They did so, and ultimately the lands thus preserved became Acadia National Park. Most of it is on Mt. Desert Island, but Schoodic Peninsula across Frenchman Bay and south of Winter Harbor is a second part, and the little seen yet soaring and glorious cliffs of Isle au Haut is a third.

Isle au Haut stands well out to sea south of Stonington. The wealthy of the cities to the south reached Isle au Haut as part of the fashionable hegira from Newport and Southampton, but Thoreau himself would quail at the remoteness of Isle au Haut and the problem of reaching the part of it that became a segment of Acadia National Park. There is a settlement called Lookout at the northern tip of the island near the best of the cliffs and something that in the name of charity might be miscalled a road around the National Park area to the south. With the admonition that one forget his high school French and call it Aisle-uh-Holt, we drop the subject.

The other central event of Mt. Desert history in our day and age was the fire of October, 1947. For four days the fire ripped through the island, utterly beyond the capacity of man to control. Fashionable Bar Harbor was almost obliterated, and thousands of acres of woodland reduced to blackened stumps. It was one of the most memorable and destructive fires of New England history. Even *Le Figaro* of Paris, normally preoccupied with Gallic concerns, pontificated about it, although the thesis advanced that the fire was set by Maine peasants in an uprising against the feudal domains of Bar Harbor has not won acceptance. But Bar Harbor and Mt. Desert Island are too blessed to rest in ashes. What has developed is a new and different island, an island of good hotels and good restaurants (in the summer, which may be defined as the period between the Fourth of July and the date in mid-October after which the foliage is no longer worth observing), and preeminently an island of good taste. It is blessedly free of honky-tonk, admirably bereft of billboards and the passage from free enterprise America into the paternalism of a national park is an easy, hardly perceptible one. The national park preserves the state of nature, but there is a state of natural good taste outside the park as well.

The essential New Jersey shore can be defined in terms of a few specific places. To define the essential Maine coast in terms of a few places, let us say of Ogunquit, Boothbay Harbor and Bar Harbor, would be entirely to miss its essence. The tip of a tongue of rock stuck into the Atlantic from the broad and rocky mainland illustrates it, but there are ten thousand such tongues in Maine. Let us take, merely by way of illustration, Pemaquid Point, the final tip of the Bristol peninsula that runs for some twenty miles south of Waldoboro. The fog is wrapped around the Point and its folds sweep and eddy in sinuous, aimless motion. The firs that creep down the Point as if to see how far the land can go in defiance of the water drip and glisten with droplets of fog. The ocean breathes and pulsates, now exhaling and the water runs up the crevices, up each sinuous rill and over the rocks as the seaweed rises and momentarily floats upon the uneasy, restless surface. Now the ocean inhales, and the water runs out of the crevices, the rills are sucked dry, the rock shakes off the ocean and the seaweed settles down in glistening, clinging wetness. The ocean is breathing gently today, as it usually does when the fog is heavy, but the power is there and it is a giant resting. The vacationist who

stands on Pemaquid Point on such a day catches the essence
of the Maine coast, but he could stand at a thousand similar
points of rock and catch it just as well. What is today, was
yesterday at places like Pemaquid Point, and will be tomorrow. Time merges with eternity, space with infinity, along
the coast of Maine.

The essence of Maine is inland just as truly as upon the
coast. Perhaps the most characteristic of all Maine vacations
has been one quite indistinguishable from a vacation in
Wisconsin or Minnesota, and so very much like one almost
anywhere on the Pacific coast as to be readily recognized.
Let us picture somewhere in Maine half a century ago a
hypothetical lake, not a massive lake like Moosehead nor an
emerald in a mountain brooch of darker green like one of the
Rangeleys, but an average lake in the average country west
of the Lewiston-Waterville line. This was the objective, and
the ride down was the prelude to the year-end dividend
which the working years for decades now have paid to the
shareholder in American life. Naturally one started from
Boston, the time-hallowed place from which to start for
Maine.

The preparations of the family with a camp on such a lake
were not overly extensive, since much of what was needed
was left at the camp over the winter. For Maine the point of
departure was the North Station, an edifice less glorious
than the South but more redolent of vacation lands beyond.
The tracks were fewer but on them were trains for the
White Mountains of New Hampshire and the Green Mountains of Vermont, and six trains a day for Montreal, as well
as trains for Maine. Our hypothetical family took the Bangor
train which made Portland with fair celerity and then
slowed down to Maine Central speed as it wound its way
through that vaguely defined piedmont in which Lewiston
and Waterville, and for that matter most of milltown Maine,
are located. The station was reached and there was waiting
in a Model T Ford a laconic friend of other summers who met
the train by arrangement and brought the rusticators to
their camp in his creaking, groaning, suddenly spurting
chariot that wheezed its way through storm and gloom of

night with all the reliability of the letter carriers of that day. The neighbor who had thus obliged was paid the sum agreed upon, with a couple of dollars above the appointed amount, an addition that was accepted but without the twitch of a muscle to admit its existence, since to acknowledge a tip would put a man in the servant class and the servant class did not exist in the State of Maine.

Anticipation had mounted as the vacationers neared the camp. What damage might the vandals have done this winter? Maine has always been full of vandals, four-footed and fur-bearing ones, and some of the worst leap from tree to tree. Then the door was opened, and the family inhaled that glorious, cold, dank, musty smell that a camp gets when it has lain there month after month with the snow banking it around and icy stalactites fringing the roof which smokes hotly on the rare day in late March when the warmth of a new year pushes into Maine. Then to the boathouse to see how the boat wintered and to scrape the pine needles off the canvas and to wonder, as they did every year, how they seep through a seemingly solid roof. Then the walk down the spongy path to the lake, the pleasantly mushy feel of the mucky ooze along the edge, the tentative extension of the palm into the water to test the warmth one knew was not there. Back in the camp, to strip the covers off the sofa and speculate on the possibility of one more season before the stuffing that was seeping through the rips became a great, disabling balloon of whatever it was they put in sofas before kapok was imported. And then the test by fire. What about the stove, and the possibility of cooking something, anything? The feeling of being Down East and the feeling of hunger had a way of coalescing. And so the day passed and the night came, and the lamps were turned down or the lights turned out depending on how deep one was in Maine, and they went to bed and listened to the strange, unidentifiable noises that the country makes at night. But not for long. Sleep came, as they rested calm in the assurance that tomorrow really started vacation, with old clothes to wear, old things to do that were forever new, old fish hooks and old lines to be readied, old tramps to be taken down old roads, old friends to see, old books to read, everything old except the feel of being Down East which is forever new, unchanged, ageless and in some strange way both placid and ecstatic. It was the vacation of the Indian Down East, not the chief but the ordinary Indian, the vacation of the American citizen who had found that one of civilization's great rewards was the right to withdraw from civilization for a time and to live a simple, wholesome, outdoors life blessedly free from the conveniences, and even more the necessities, of modern life. When the necessities were no longer necessary, then one was really on vacation in the State of Maine.

It is precisely the same today, in Maine and in that extension of the Maine littoral, landscape and philosophy of living, New Brunswick, and with modifications and exceptions in the provinces beyond. Let us move farther Down East.

Half a century ago the boats to Down East rivaled in importance the boats to Maine, and in the minds of many surpassed it. There were two boats Down East from Boston, the St. John boat already mentioned and the Yarmouth boat. The Yarmouth boat was the really important one. Boston has always been the first port of call for Nova Scotians seeking employment, and it has been estimated that at least a million Massachusetts residents are of Canadian Maritime birth or descent, with Nova Scotia the leading contributor. Indeed there are still Bostonians to whom *Nova Scotia* is a generic term applied to all eastern Canada, which may be a bit of geographic misinformation but, more interestingly, may be a survival from the days before Confederation when there was political justification for such use.

Only in such geometric areas as the midwestern states do the four points of the compass have a thoroughly useful meaning. There can be no reasonable doubt of the location of South Dakota vis-à-vis North Dakota. There is every reason to be careful about the location of Nova Scotia vis-à-vis Massachusetts. Nova Scotia is a huge peninsula, linked to the mainland far north of Boston but stretching south until it reaches Yarmouth, a point about opposite Portland, Maine.

It is farther from Boston to Yarmouth than it is to Portland, but not as much farther as one might imagine nor did it take the Yarmouth boat much longer to reach its destination than it did the Portland boat. On the other hand, by land Yarmouth is very nearly as far from Boston as Boston is from Chicago and with the railroad service what it was to that neck of the woods even in its heyday, the ride by train to Yarmouth seemed of Trans-Siberian proportions. It was a pleasant afternoon and night sail by boat, and no one ever dreamed of going any other way. Since Nova Scotia is the homeland to so many Bostonians, and since it is blessed with one of the best summer climates this side of Hawaii, there was much to be said for reserving your stateroom well in advance during July and August.

There was no way fifty years ago of softening the travel blow for the person homeward bound or vacation bound to the most scenic part of Nova Scotia, Cape Breton Island. One might take the boat to Yarmouth, if he chose, but beyond there stretched endless miles of railroad ties and trains of philosophic leisure. The boat to St. John served one no better since the glories of Canadian railroading, the Canadian Pacific and the Grand Trunk, were not to be had Down East save with "the excess of glory obscured." One's deepest grief, however, had to be reserved for the hapless if dauntless soul homeward bound for Newfoundland, for in those days no one ventured to that remote and questionably hyperborean realm save the homecoming native.

For the wayfarer who chose the rugged longueurs of train travel Down East, *train* meant The Gull. The Gull was a train to conjure with. It pulled out of the North Station on the Boston & Maine tracks each evening except Saturday. If it left on Saturday it would be in Nova Scotia on Sunday, and legend had it that the strict exegetes of Nova Scotia Calvinism held that the Sabbath movement of railroad trains was morally illicit. Whether this was legend or libel the writer does not know, and he is willing to let it rest somewhere between the two.

The Gull was a train to everywhere north and east of Boston. The unit was not the train but the car. One might be

on the Aroostook car, the St. John car, the Halifax car, the
car for the Prince Edward Island ferry, but if one was
heading for Cape Breton Island or for Newfoundland he had
to change at Truro for the Sydney car. The Gull wheeled its
leisurely way through Maine, New Brunswick and Nova
Scotia, moulting cars as it went. The cars that endured to the
end were ferried across the Strait of Canso onto Cape Breton
Island and came at last to North Sydney and the dock. Here
the voyager to Cape Breton might rest, but not the homing
Newfoundlander. For him the horrors of rail travel to this
tip of Cape Breton Island was but the prelude. Beyond lay a
night crossing of waters that would make Shakespeare's
"still-vex'd Bermoothes" resemble the swanboat lagoon in
the Boston Public Garden, and beyond that the delights of
twenty-four hours on the narrow gauge train that curved in
a magnificent arch high up into Newfoundland, and then
down again to St. John's. Portal to portal from Boston took
all or part of four distinct days. There was no way of
shortening the time, although the horrors could be eliminated if one took the Furness Line boat which offered
regular service between Boston and Liverpool, with stops at
Halifax and St. John's. It was a leisurely and comfortable
way to Newfoundland, and indeed to England, but speed was
never claimed for it nor sought by it. Furness never forgot
that Rome was not built in a day nor Liverpool reached in a
week. The airplane, like all blessings, is mixed but it comes
closer to unmixed purity where Cape Breton and Newfoundland are concerned than about any other place one might
mention in eastern America. Only veterans of the safari by
rail to those arctic outposts can appreciate to the full the
blessing that Air Canada now bestows with its comfortable
and rapid service from Boston to all major points Down East.

There is more than a touch of nostalgia to the recollection
of all these boats out of Boston, the New Orleans boat with a
real show of luxury to its appointments, the finely furnished
and highly serviceable Merchant and Miner boats to Philadelphia, Baltimore and Norfolk, the Furness boats to Liverpool via Down East which gave freighter travel at its
comfortable best, and even the overnight boats to Maine that

were built and equipped with an unceasing awareness that a night on the bounding main does not last forever and that Eastern Steamship was not in competition for the carriage trade with Cunard and North German Lloyd. The cabins were cribbed and confined, the bunks were of monastic hardness, the washing facilities were designed for the more dwarfish Lilliputians and the conviction of the ship designers that passengers traveled without luggage was unshakeable. The day of the side paddle had not entirely departed although the screw-driven craft was rapidly taking over, and the sight of the massive, gleaming pistons rhythmically rising and falling as seen through plate glass windows installed for passenger edification and instruction had a way of losing its fascination in the light of the cumbersome and sluggish plod that resulted.

But all this was nothing compared to the compensation the boats to Maine or Down East offered. They offered to everyone with a five- or a ten-dollar bill in his pocket what the contemporary cruise offers to the person with an American Express credit card backed up by fiscal soundness thoroughly deserving of credit. They offered very much less of it and certainly nothing suggesting comparable quality, but no one offers anything like it today in Boston or New York or any city one may name. And perhaps they offered something in even greater quantity than the finest cruise ship afloat now can offer. They offered that thrill, impossible to define and impossible to mistake, of feeling that one was sailing out of the workaday world into a world of romance, the thrill of watching the Custom House Tower, which then soared high above Boston's modest skyline, gradually fade into dim indistinctness and in the mind's eye the towers of Carcassonne and the minarets of Samarkand take its place. In the literal world these towers and minarets were merely Portland City Hall, the Bangor House, the fringe of structures along Yarmouth harbor, but they were such only in the literal world where the natives lived. To the vacationer, whose money was earned by far harder work than today puts afloat the matron and her retired husband on the cruise ship to North Cape, and to whom two weeks Down East was a luxury dreamed of, scrimped for and now just taking shape as the outer islands of Boston harbor slip by and then Nix's Mate and Boston Light, and beyond the open ocean without dimensions, boundaries or end, those two weeks were as close to heaven as one reaches on earth, and the swish of the water and the slosh of the paddles might well be the sweep of angels' wings as one crossed the great void between fifty weeks of reality and two weeks of romance. There was never a better way to start them than leaning over the rail of a boat steaming out through Boston harbor on a perfectly still, perfectly clear, late August evening. No one has come up with a better way since.

8. Macadam and the model T

All the vacations considered hitherto have been vacations in the state of rest, with travel incidental even when travel was so precious in itself as it was on an Eastern Steamship or a Merchant and Miner vessel. But vacation has not always been limited to a beatific state of rest. The Grand Tour also has an illustrious tradition, and nineteenth-century Americans, appropriately vestured and otherwise outfitted and with means commensurate with the Grand Tour at its noblest, made the tour of the European capitals in the ancient and honorable fashion. As the twentieth century gathered momentum the Grand Tour was appropriately trimmed down for those whose vesture, outfitting and fiscal competence were to some degree modified, but except for the college student who by rigid tradition had to work his way across on a cattle boat—no craft of less olfactory impact was deemed appropriate—there was always something grand in cost as well as scope to a European trip. Nothing quite comparable to the Grand Tour ever developed in the United States, possibly because such state capitals as Pierre, Bismarck and Carson City are at a cultural and historical disadvantage in the competition with London, Paris and Rome and possibly because cultural and historical disadvantages have a way of being translated into disadvantages of prestige. Prestige has always been a treasured by-product of the Grand Tour whether taken by an Englishman or an American.

The American and Canadian railroads did their best to

bring a Grand Tour into being, the Santa Fe depending heavily on the Grand Canyon and the Canadian Pacific countering with Banff and Lake Louise. The Union Pacific was never quite so well off, since its founding fathers had prudently by-passed the worst of the Rocky Mountains, leaning heavily on the gently modulating uplands of Wyoming, but it did establish a beachhead on Utah scenery at Ogden and beyond lay California and all that connoted. Beauty was the traveler's excuse for being on the less fiscally endowed Rio Grande Western and its scion the Western Pacific that forced their way through the heart of the Colorado Rockies, threaded the Utah desert, glided in the friendly silence of the moonlight through the empty reaches of Nevada and sinuously coasted down the Feather River Canyon to a modest harborage at Oakland, on the wrong side of the Bay. Be their liabilities what they may have been, and the liabilities the Rockies saddle on a railroad in winter are monumental, they had the scenery and they gave the best Grand Tour of the Rockies that was possible on rails. We mention all this because even in the American Grand Tour by rail the travel was usually a means to an end, the end being an entranced state of rest beside Lake Louise or of awe-stricken wonder as one leaned over a railing and looked a mile or so down into the Grand Canyon. Only the DRGW-WP route made the travel the primary end in itself, and even that was climaxed by a ferry ride across the Bay to the American city most like the storied cities of romance, San Francisco.

Change, however, is the ultimate essence of existence, as the philosopher Heraclitus made verbosely clear some twenty-five hundred years ago. It was a change when vacation for many ceased to be spent in a state of rest and began to be spent in a state of travel. This was not the basic change, however, since it was a change that affected a minority and, furthermore, there was behind it the long and noble tradition of the Grand Tour. The basic change came when vacation became a state of travel in a vehicle propelled by the owner and occupied by his family, and hence totally within his jurisdiction and control. It was the tour in the family car, not the tour on the railroad train, which changed the fundamental pattern. Behind this change were two men, John Louden McAdam and Henry Ford.

John McAdam had already lived when our period dawned, and Henry Ford was in his prime. In 1815 McAdam had proved that when successive layers of progressively smaller stones are laid on a firm base of large stones, then a crushed rock surface laid on them and finally a mixture of stone dust and water placed on top, the whole business hardens and a paved road is the result. One hundred years later Henry Ford proved that a self-propelled vehicle, simple in design, sturdy in construction and reliable in operation can be turned out by methods of mass production and the average man can be given a means of mechanical self-propulsion as practical from the economic viewpoint as from the scientific. Thus one of the most ancient dreams of the human race, the dream that had been changed into a limited reality by James Watt and his inspiration which developed ultimately in the locomotive and the train, became reality and with it an utterly new and unprecedented pattern for the vacation. To say this is an obvious reduction of something monumental in significance to a limited application, a reduction so drastic as to smack of the absurd. The combination of McAdam and Ford brought into being an utterly new and unprecedented pattern for life, and proved as it has been proved so often in history that a mechanic tinkering with machinery in a shed as he brings into being a new idea may do infinitely more to change the pattern of life than all the statesmen that ever lived.

We take good roads for granted, or more exactly we complain loudly and bitterly when good roads are not perfect. Let us turn back to a day when in the currently accepted sense there were no roads at all. America probably had better highways in 1773 than in 1873, and certainly had better ones in 1843 when eighty turnpike companies were operating in Pennsylvania, 278 companies in New York and New England had 3,754 miles of good turnpike roads. The older generation in Massachusetts to this day calls U.S. 1 north of Boston the Newburyport Turnpike and State 9 the Worcester Pike, although I-95 has largely replaced the one and a modern toll road parallels the other. With no consciousness of inconsistency the toll road beside the Worcester Pike is called "The Mass Pike." But the turnpikes largely passed into oblivion in the half century after 1843. In 1873, when the railroad was supreme, the United States and Canada needed roads of two kinds, city streets and feeder roads to the railroad station. Plank roads were fine for the latter purpose, as highways were made obsolete by the railroads.

In 1873 what are today U.S. 20, 30 and 40, or if one prefers I-90, 80 and 70, to the extent that the lineage of these highways admits of tracing, were a set of badly decayed trails over one rock ridge down into the next mudhole, in and around every obstacle that nature and man had thrown in their path, but creeping, crawling, paddling and swimming on until they reached Chicago. They were the vestigial remains of an outmoded past and as the passenger rode in plush luxury on the New York Central, the Pennsylvania or the Baltimore and Ohio he might catch a fleeting glimpse of some farmer with his shoulder to the wagon wheel and never suspect that he was watching tomorrow being born as he rode the Twentieth Century or the Capitol Limited to oblivion. Then came the bicycle.

Shortly after 1873 Colonel Albert A. Pope began to make bicycles in the United States, and made a modest living from them. The great breakthrough came in England in 1885, when a low-wheeled bicycle with gears was developed. Colonel Pope saw at once the superiority of construction and the comparative safety that the low-wheeled bicycle afforded, and saw as well its supreme merit. A woman could ride it. A woman could ride it, that is, if there was a road fit for her to ride. Unlike the air which dictates the designing of the airplane, and the water which ordains the structure of the boat, or for that matter the parallel irons which impose a fundamental structure on the railroad train, it is the vehicle which determines the principle of construction of a highway and not the other way around. The bicycle requires a smooth surface with the attainable minimum of hills, but the road need not be wide. Instigated by cyclists and their needs the first good roads movement after the surge of toll-road building in the early nineteenth century was started in 1892 with the formation of a National League for Good Roads and the creation the next year of an Office of Road Inquiry in the Department of Agriculture. The Office, which had a budget of ten thousand dollars to finance its inquiries, was dedicated to "lifting our people out of the mud," and presumably Agriculture was its appropriate department since mud is an aspect of landscape and since roads existed not merely for bicyclists but far more for farmers en route to market. The roads that were paved were built with bicyclists in mind and tended to be narrow. Roads built for wagons were wide, since wagons must be turned.

By 1904 the Office of Road Inquiry had unearthed these truths: the United States had 2,151,570 miles of road of which 153,662 were improved. Improvement was a word of unsurpassed flexibility. Most of it was euphemistic for gravel covering; 38,622 miles were surfaced with water-bound macadam and other forms of improvement were achieved with surfaces of sand, shell or planks. Practically all the surfacing that might be considered good by modern standards was in Ohio, which had 104 miles of America's 123 miles of brick surfacing and sixteen of the nation's eighteen miles of bituminous macadam or asphalt. The fundamental fact was never lost sight of where road building was concerned: a good road was a road which enabled the farmer to get expeditiously from farm to market or railhead, not a highway that brought a traveler from city to city. Roads existed to supplement railways and were built at right angles to the railroad right of way, intersecting with it at railroad stations and freight depots. But as the new century dawned the automobile was a growing cloud of dust on the roads of America, ninety-four percent of which were plain dirt, abundantly rich in dust when Nature smiled and in mud when Nature wept. On July 28, 1897, Alexander Winton left Cleveland by automobile and following what is now the route of I-90 and the New York Thruway reached New York City on August 7. The omens and portents were there, for those who would see them.

By 1910 it was obvious that the automobile and not the

The Sunday drive afforded limitless opportunities for al fresco dining.

bicycle was the individual's vehicle of the future, and at about that date the era of the modern highway began. The Model T Ford was now a factor in American life and it soon became clear that the dimensions of the factor were destined to stagger the most resilient imagination. Another fact to conjure with was emerging: it was becoming clear that the motor-driven truck and not the horse-drawn wagon was the efficient and economical conveyance of freight for distances between twenty and fifty miles. But there was a distinction between the Model T Ford and its compeers on the one hand and the truck on the other that was destined to cause a massive divergence for a time. The truck was designed to serve an economic purpose, and it served it most economically for some years as a farm-to-market or -to-railhead vehicle. The truck ran on feeder roads built at right angles to the railroad, and indeed the railroads, quite unaware of the potential dimensions of the camel they were inviting into the tent, gladly sponsored the building of feeder roads to replace unprofitable branch lines. The truck as an intercity competitor to the railroad was still a cloud on the horizon no bigger than a brakeman's hand.

The Model T, on the other hand, was termed a "pleasure car." The two-seated, open-top model was a "touring car." There is nothing snide or derogatory implied in the use of quotation marks. For a long time the vehicle with a flat body in which merchandise was packed was destined for an exclusively business function; the day of the station wagon belonged to an unsuspected future. Far more important, the vehicle with seats for people was designed for pleasure and was used for pleasure driving. Pleasure driving at first was limited in scope, mainly the Sunday afternoon drive or the drive in the cool of the summer's evening. The most practical form the vehicle took was the family-sized car that seated five persons, two in the front seat and three in the rear and did so with an intensity of squeezing not too much greater than is customary in the modern airplane.

In its name, touring car, lay the promise and the challenge. The truck went from farm to market or railhead, but the touring car went from town to town. Two entirely different types of road were involved. The truck required a road at right angles to the railroad, a pleasure car a road that paralleled the railroad. The truck supplemented the railroad, the pleasure car competed with it. The result was a basic debate which came to a head in 1916 when the Federal Aid Road Act was passed: Should feeder roads be improved for trucks or should highways be built for pleasure cars? The compromise effected was an appropriation of seventy-five million dollars to be spent in five years on rural post roads by the Secretary of Agriculture, the appropriation to be matched fifty-fifty by the states. As we have seen, the road system that actually existed in 1916 resembled much more closely a series of feelers extending out from the railroad lines than a network of highways crisscrossing the country. Most roads existed to bring produce to market or railhead, and farms were structured in terms of the delivery of produce. Hence the chief impact of the Act was to improve the road system that already existed, since the mail went out to the farms, but a fair amount of what might be termed highway improvement did result from the Act. But 1917 was a year utterly different from 1916, and war was destined to turn a page in the nation's book of economics and start a new chapter.

Before 1917 was over the railroads of America had ground to a halt under the most monumental traffic jam in American history. Freight cars clogged every available siding and so backed up onto main lines as to threaten total paralysis of the railroad system. The government took over the railroads and the Council for National Defense in a desperate move to extemporize an adjunct to the rail system created a Highway Transport Committee headed by Roy D. Chapin. He had an inspiration and the courage to carry it through, and the success of his inspiration provides another proof that the strikingly successful idea can lose through success the entire aura of originality. His idea was to have trucks driven under their own power to shipboard rather than conveyed on freight cars, and he embellished the inspiration by having the trucks loaded with merchandise. In the dead of the winter of 1917 a convoy of thirty trucks set out on the perilous land voyage from Detroit to Baltimore, a voyage that carried them through the inhospitable wilderness of the Alleghenies, into the heart of darkest Pennsylvania. Twenty-nine of them made it. By Armistice Day in 1918, eighteen thousand trucks had made it and America had made a discovery. A truck may be more than a complement to a railroad car. It may be a competitor. Furthermore, a truck and a pleasure car need not be competitors over the issue of feeder road versus highway. They may be collaborators in the holy cause of highway funds. Germany lost the First World War, and so did the American railroads, although years would pass before the fact of defeat would be apparent.

Our concern is still the touring car. We have already met the redoubtable Alexander Winton who in 1897 made the traverse perilous from Cleveland to New York in eleven short days. In 1901 Roy D. Chapin added nearly two hundred miles to Winton's distance and cut over three days from his time when he drove his Merry Oldsmobile from Detroit to New York in seven-and-one-half days. He took the route north of Lake Erie from Detroit to Niagara Falls and then prudently used the towpath of the Erie Canal across upstate New York on the reasonable grounds that it was much smoother and made for better driving than the roads from city to city. His hour of glory was brief. Before the year was out the Apperson brothers of now sadly diminished Haynes-Apperson fame drove from Kokomo, Indiana, to New York in seven days. One might note that these hardy pioneers of the machine age might start anywhere but their destination was New York, even as the destination of Colonel Lindbergh and his successors, whether reached or not reached, was Paris. This was still the golden age of the railroad, but it was also the golden age of the city which the railroad had done so much to make.

There was another destination quite as alluring as New York and hypothetically at least far more difficult to attain. The drive from New York to the Pacific coast was as obvious as the nonstop flight across the Atlantic to Paris. Three transcontinental trips were completed in 1903, one in as few as fifty-three days. The Wild West may have sounded more ominous, but it was no worse than the mud-clogged East. Thus the fact was established that it was possible to cross America by auto. The fact had been established with equal clarity that it was possible only with extreme difficulty and only by men of undeviating resolution, uncompromising dedication to a cause, strong arm and thigh muscles, a way with balky machinery and a faculty for getting tires off wheels in a day before that invaluable and now blithely assumed adjunct to driving had been invented, the demountable rim. Much could be done about the problems of the auto by automotive engineers, but there was also much that could be done by highway crews. It was the glory of Carl Graham Fisher who founded the Prest-O-Lite Company to propose it: a paved highway from coast to coast, to be called the Lincoln Highway. The idea caught on and a short-lived Lincoln Highway Association was formed. The idea outlived the Association, and ultimately U.S. 30 from Atlantic City to Astoria, Oregon, came into being as the Lincoln Highway. Today it is superseded in the main by various units of the interstate system, but a certain aura still surrounds its name, just as a certain aura surrounds such railroad names as Union Pacific and Canadian Pacific, such a steamship name as Cunard, and it may be but it is too early to tell, such an airplane name as Boeing 747. There is a romance to the road, whether the road is a highway dipping below the horizon on the western plains, the parallels of a railroad line merging in the hazy distance, the furrow of a ship building its foaming road that slowly ripples down to an indistinct calm far astern or the chalk mark of a jet slashed across the blue of a morning sky. A name like Lincoln Highway rings with romance, and not all the traffic lights on U.S. 30 can blind one to the thrill of knowing that this highway, which is no different from other highways in appearance and very much less a highway than the ones built in recent years, is one of the abiding monuments of America's progress.

By 1920 the family car was a major factor in American life. In 1900 one American in 9,499 owned an auto, in 1910 one in 201, in 1920 one in thirteen. The auto was no longer the exclusive possession of the athlete-mechanic, or the rich man who could hire the athlete-mechanic-chauffeur, but had become as well the property of the average man with his average, modest objectives in life. There are ventures in locomotion for the sturdiest of spirit and for the most subdued, but the emotional response to the massive achievement and the modest achievement does not bear a necessary relationship to massiveness and modesty. It was a day when one could drive across the country with a fair expectation of seeing the Pacific from the family touring car, but it was also a day when the great majority of families got a thrill that no one can get today from a modest venture into the country, a night spent here and a night spent there with a change of scenery every day and even every hour, and an enjoyment in this new kind of vacation that people talked about but really had to be experienced to be appreciated. Americans were not to know a similar thrill until the recent inauguration by the airlines of one-week trips to Europe. A younger generation must take on faith the statement that the drive from Boston over the Mohawk Trail in western Massachusetts and on to Albany had in 1920 the kind of emotional impact that the flight across the ocean and over the Alps to Rome has today.

There are two basic ways to talk about the 1920 vacation in the touring car and only two. One is to do so in statistical terms: so many cars, so many drivers, so many roads, so much progress in paving roads, so much improvement in road-building technique. One can cover the nation this way, but it is a cold, impersonal way as befits what Carlyle called the dismal science. The other way is to talk about the actual vacation trips taken from a particular starting point and in a particular region, and to do so with the understanding that a book of nostalgia is by its nature a cooperative enterprise, and that the reader must complete from his own memory, or perhaps from his own sympathetic imagination, the equations that the writer can only suggest. One thing is certain: no driver could conceivably cover the country in the 1920s as one can in the 1970s, and no driver did. One can write about touring in a particular state fifty years ago, or a particular group of states, but not about touring in the United States.

This country is just too big, roads were just too bad and autos just too undependable, not to say uncomfortable.

We start from Boston, the only place in those days from which the writer ever started. There was the drive to and from Cape Cod, a drive to be taken within the span of a single day and so illustrative of the vacation drive rather than a true example of it. The streetcar was an omnipresent fact of life in the 1920s, and one could court ennui by following it or disaster by trying to pass it. Hypothetically one could pass it on the right, but with one American in thirteen owning an auto he would be sure to park it by the curb of a street with streetcars. Motoring has offered no more subtle problem in time, rate and distance than the sprint past a moving streetcar with a parked auto looming ever closer and closer.

The streetcar line from Boston petered out in Quincy and thereafter you wound your leisurely way down the South Shore of Massachusetts, made the more leisurely in fact but not in mental attitude by the Sunday driver who headed at the sedate pace of twenty miles an hour an ever lengthening line of autos following the leader in dogged despair. Every now and then, with blessed unexpectedness, the Sunday driver would turn down a side road and a shudder of vibrant life would ripple down the line and motors roar as the left pedal was pushed down and the Model T leaped forward to savor its unanticipated freedom. (For the more recently born, the Model T Ford had a planetary transmission, engaged in low gear by depressing the left pedal and eased into high gear by letting the pedal out. The middle pedal made the car go backwards and the right pedal was the brake. The accelerator was a metallic rod projecting to the right of the steering wheel and operated by the driver's right hand. Projecting to the left was another rod called the spark, a rod to be depressed and the spark thereby retarded before the car was cranked. The penalty for neglect could be a broken arm.)

One wound his already mentioned leisurely way down the South Shore of Massachusetts, made leisurely to a fault as one reached Plymouth and a standstill. It is the writer's unshakeable conviction that no traffic jam conjured by the perversities of this modern age can touch the traffic jams that Plymouth, Massachusetts, could brew on pleasant Sundays fifty years ago. There was in the early New England genius an instinct for the sparing approach to life's resources. The mere fact that an empty continent stretched to the Pacific Ocean was no reason for the Pilgrims to use more of that continent than was necessary on the main street of Plymouth. One endured through Plymouth, buoyed by the thought of Cape Cod beyond and by the knowledge that there were other ways back to Boston, even if the best of them perforce included the highway horrors of Brockton itself. But one reached Bourne, crossed the old bridge over the canal and was on Cape Cod. There delight began.

There are two shores to Cape Cod, and they are as different as the shores of this vale of tears from the shores of light. The bay shore is where the migrant Pilgrims settled and put a mark upon the land crystal clear to this day. A street of old and gracious houses, and of trees that have spread their protecting arms over street and houses for three hundred years, gently winds through Sandwich, Barnstable, Yarmouth, Dennis and Brewster as it makes its placid way toward Orleans and Chatham, loveliest of Cape towns and the crazy bone at the Cape's elbow. It was a joy to drive fifty years ago, and it is still the same joy to drive today. There are motels on it now, but they are small and in good taste, and business is not big enough to warrant shopping centers. Besides, business is mostly where the towns thin out and the road becomes country. Fifty years ago the road that now is called U.S. 6A was exclusively a road to yesterday, fifty miles from Boston and at least two hundred years away. A day on such a road, and there were many such with similar or comparable charms throughout America, was a totally new and unprecedented vacation thrill half a century ago, and it was the Model T which made the thrill possible for the one American in thirteen who owned a car and the four other Americans he invited for the ride. Today a business man can fly a thousand miles to Chicago, transact his business and be back in Boston and in bed by midnight. Fifty years ago he could drive to the seventeenth century and be back home in Boston and in bed by midnight, if the traffic jam in Brockton was not too great. Is two thousand miles necessarily farther than two hundred years?

Then there were the overnight trips out of Boston. There was the trip to New York, a pleasure trip if *pleasure* is meticulously defined and limited in its application. In those days New York really was Fun City, but the pleasure was in being there, not in getting there. Theoretically one was supposed to drive down to Providence, wriggle around the shore to New London and then slow down in towns and speed up between them until one reached New Haven and the grim and endless miles of city traffic from there to the Grand Concourse and Manhattan beyond. The other way was to drive by Worcester but through Springfield, and then down the far from unpopulated Connecticut Valley to New Haven and the ensuing horrors. In practice Bostonians and New Yorkers collaborated in working out a diagonal route called the Stafford Springs route after the sedate and ancient watering place which was the one oasis between Worcester and Hartford. What motorists worked out for themselves highway engineers finally accepted, and the modern derivative of the Stafford Springs route is now the accepted route between Boston and New York, with the accolade of an interstate route number. But even the Stafford Springs route left to be faced the ultimate challenge: New Haven, Bridgeport, Stamford, New Rochelle and all the lesser but far from inconsiderable habitations of man which made U.S. 1 through Connecticut and New York a driver's nightmare and left immovable the conviction that if one American in thirteen owned a car, he drove it on U.S. 1 in Connecticut every Sunday. Let no one belittle the traffic jams that were possible a half century ago. The writer recalls the pleasant summer Sunday when he left Danbury, Connecticut, at dawn and drove from dawn to noon, from noon to dewy eve and at dewy eve was in Princeton, New Jersey. Today he should be in Charleston, South Carolina. But New York was worth it, in those days. Indeed it was.

Next there were the longer drives with scenery the

objective. The two most favored ones from Boston were to the White Mountains and over the Mohawk Trail. The White Mountains, in addition to their other charms, are blessed with one practical advantage that was invaluable in the days when touring was young and venturesome: they have notches, not passes. You may drive the main north-south notches, Franconia and Pinkham, on roads amazingly close to level considering the mountainous country you are penetrating, and the same is reasonably close to true of the most spectacular of the notches, the diagonal Crawford Notch. This was an unmixed blessing in the days when all hills were challenges and some hills demanded the most heroic measure of all if one was driving a Model T, namely, a complete turnabout of the car and an ascent of the hill backwards. What the mechanical principle involved may have been the writer does not know, but his memory is clarity itself on the basic fact: there were hills so steep that a Model T would not go up frontwards but would go up backwards. It may have been that the car was stalled in frontwards position by malnutrition, since the gasoline reached the engine by gravity from a tank beneath the front seat. When a car ascends a hill backwards, the engine is inevitably lower than the front seat if the engine is where historically the engine has been. On the other hand it may have been that the reverse gear, which the improvident used as a second brake when the regular brake was excessively worn as it habitually was, had a gear ratio of greater climbing ability than the forward gear. But the main roads through the White Mountains made no such demands on the ability of a driver to make a fresh and agonized appraisal of a driving problem and then carry through successfully a solution in the reversal of every sane canon of locomotion.

The White Mountains are known to all if for no other reason than the fact that the Old Man of the Mountains is there in eternal profile. The Mohawk Trail, on the other hand, may require definition. A tribe of Indians, the Mohawks, centuries before the birth of the Model T, used to make their way over the top of the Berkshires and down the sides all the way from the Hudson Valley to the Connecticut

An advertisement, circa 1910.

Valley. After the white man came the Indians continued to do it, to the great discomfiture of the Connecticut Valley white man in general and the people of Deerfield, Massachusetts, in particular. The Indian forays culminated in the Deerfield massacre of 1704. Peace later settled over the Berkshires and by and large has remained there since, as has the Mohawk Trail. Widened, paved, progressively accommodated with restaurants, gift shops and tourist cabins immortalizing the name of the Mohawks, it is by general assent the premier tourist road and scenic attraction of Massachusetts, becoming on autumn weekends when foliage is at its peak a snake dance of autos from end to end. As time went on and highways became methodized it was christened State 2, but no one calls it that except where it is an office-to-bedroom road for historic suburbia like Lexington and Concord. Strictly speaking, however, it is the Mohawk Trail only for the sixty-three miles between the Connecticut River near Greenfield and the New York line. It has always been a fine road to drive and it still is, as it rises on its twisting path through ravines and gorges of the refined Massachusetts sort to a splendid pair of climaxes, an eastern overlook at the Savoy State Forest which gives one to imagine that Massachusetts is a virgin wilderness and a western outlook at Hairpin Turn, a nice bit of switchback road with a parking area and a view of North Adams far below and the sometimes quiet groves of academe at Williamstown, and up the valley to the right a view into the state of Vermont. Today it is a slower but more scenic way to Albany than the Mass Pike, but a half century ago it was an adventure and an achievement. Some friends of motoring man placed strategic barrels of water at the steeper rises, that overlaboring motors might be refreshed; those sagacious in the ways of the Trail plotted strategy involving resting places and the harboring of motive power for the final push through a hamlet called of all things, Florida, to the Elks Statue and the eastern overlook. The Elks Statue and the eastern overlook were the crowning glory of the drive and the supreme achievement; Hairpin Turn and the view up and down the valley were the reward. There was, of course, also the true reward, the boast that one had made the Mohawk Trail.

A driver could continue into New York, across the Taconics to Albany, and then down the Hudson where further glories and tests of derring-do awaited him. The best was to be built later, the old Storm King Highway, a crack of road hacked out along the side of a rock cliff high above the Hudson near West Point. Today its glory is diminished and its fame obscured by the effortless and yet scenic glide along the New York Thruway, well and safely in from the edge of the cliff, but the Storm King still lives. It is known modestly as State 218 and it still goes to West Point. There was also that paragon of bridges, the Bear Mountain Bridge, with its fine approaches down which one eased the car and felt a surge of unselfish joy that the passengers at least could look at the scenery. Boston to New York was a two-day journey that way, and worth every minute of it.

There was another trip, longer, more venturesome, with the added fillip of the foreign, the trip to Montreal and Quebec. There were two basic ways to Quebec, through the White Mountains and up the Jackman road. We have been to the White Mountains; the Jackman road was something else again. Time was, as those still able to get about reckon time, when the pavement in Maine stopped at Brunswick and anything the effete would call civilization stopped at Skowhegan. Beyond were the Maine woods, a phrase to be used with respect and one calculated to thrill the user. Not far from Skowhegan one entered the Maine woods, and kept rising, falling, twisting, turning and forever plunging into deeper woods on a narrow, dusty, bumpy road varied by wider stretches which had a few houses and bore names like Solon, Bingham, Caratunk, West Forks, Lake Parlin and Jackman Station. Somewhere beyond Jackman and the customs officers the traveler made a final wooded twist and was aware that "his luminous home of waters opens, wide and tranquil. . . ." He was out of the Maine woods and in the placid, level valley of the Chaudiere River in Quebec, a foreign land but a pleasant, smiling one with reassuring farmhouses always visible and fine dirt roads that had been carefully graded and were conscientiously dragged. Beyond were Levis and the ferry to Quebec which crossed the great, majestic river of North America, the St. Lawrence, and beyond the ferry the soaring rock that is crowned by the most majestic of hotels, the Chateau Frontenac, and the citadel beyond and above. There were other ways to Quebec and there still are, but the best way for a first visit is by ferry from Levis.

Today the motorist has the choice of routes between Quebec and Montreal that he so often has between major cities, the choice between the high-speed, contemporary highway that offers no driving problems, no delays, no difficulties and no interest, and the old road that hugs the river, winds through towns, is slow, troublesome, exasperating and fascinating. Life was simpler then and there was no chance to make the wrong choice. One was slowed, troubled, exasperated and fascinated by the drive from Quebec to Montreal. One had to come back to Boston, as one always has to from vacation wherever one's Boston may be. One long, slow way that eked out a few more golden hours and so had much to recommend it was directly south from Montreal to Rouses Point in New York and then down through Plattsburg, Glens Falls, Saratoga Springs, Albany, the Taconic Trail, the Mohawk Trail and so to Boston and to work on Monday morning. One had to stop overnight somewhere, and the best somewhere was Saratoga Springs. Then there was the choice of ways from Montreal through Vermont. All roads went through gulfs, as notches are called in Vermont, all were beautiful, all were dirt, all were rough. In those days all Vermont roads were rough and beautiful. Today they are smooth and beautiful. The adventure is gone from a drive through Vermont but the beauty remains, and beauty and Vermont come as close to being synonyms as this fair land presents.

All this is in terms of driving out of Boston, as such driving was a half century ago. The term *half century* is used in the Pickwickian sense, to mean the twenty years between

1910 and 1930, but especially the second decade. Any book of nostalgia, as we have said, must by its nature be a cooperative enterprise, with the reader doing his share of the reminiscing. America was full of Bostons half a century ago from which one could go on modest tours, Bostons with names like New York, Philadelphia, Pittsburgh, Cleveland, Chicago, St. Louis, Omaha, Denver, Salt Lake City, San Francisco. For the New Yorker there were the near and hospitable Catskills and the more remote and venturesome Adirondacks. For him and the Philadelphian there were the whole coast of New Jersey and the nearby Poconos as well. There were for others the woods and trout streams of central and western Pennsylvania, the blue-green hills of western Maryland, Virginia and West Virginia, and the higher and hazier hills of North Carolina beyond. There were the shores of Lake Huron and Lake Michigan, the ferry ride across Mackinac (and often the endless wait for the ferry as well), and beyond was a virgin land for those venturesome enough to tour the upper peninsula. There were the comfortable Missouri Ozarks and the Ouachita and Ozark regions of Arkansas beyond, where south meets west and the two form a land that is part of both and therefore different from either. Beyond were the Rockies, always beckoning to Denver and Salt Lake City, and one could choose among the glories at San Francisco, those to the north and south, and those to the east. All these were waiting to be toured, some more venturesome than others but all with rich attractions of their own. But this is the point at which the reader must weave from memory the fabric of recollection personal to himself. These were the years when an entirely new pattern of vacation was worked out, a pattern essentially American and Canadian, a travel pattern that was a tour but nothing like the Grand Tour which is an ancient European tradition.

It is time for Dr. Gradgrind to resume his work. Even before our two germinal decades certain features of the modern highway were beginning to appear. The city street with a dividing center strip is at least as old as 1903 when Philadelphia started the North East Boulevard, later rechristened the Roosevelt Boulevard. The road was from the start imposing and dignified, with its sixty-foot central drive, its thirty-four-foot service roads flanking the drive and the footpaths and planted areas between. The traffic circle would seem to be continental in origin, with the French back in 1906 working out on paper not merely the traffic circle but also the grade separation for intersecting highways and the links constructed on the cloverleaf principle. An American, Arthur Hale of Maryland, actually got a patent for the concept in 1916. London also, with its penchant for law and possibly its continuing penchant for fast driving, was drafting "Gyratory Traffic Regulations" by at least 1907, a phrase later simplified to traffic circle. Then there are the circles of Washington, D.C., that were instrumentalities of defense in intent and of traffic control in reality.

On the whole, New Jersey was the state which did the most pioneer work in what we consider modern highway construction, and considering New Jersey traffic well it might have. The first traffic circle in America outside city limits was at Woodbridge. Blending routes 4 and 25, it was built in 1928. The road from Elizabeth to the Holland Tunnel provided a cluster of firsts: limited access, the covered cut and that quondam marvel of elevated highway the wonder of which no later highway has ever entirely eclipsed, the Pulaski Skyway. It was not, however, a divided highway and there were relatively few such until after World War II. Route 9 from Boston to Worcester, Massachusetts, already referred to as the Worcester Pike and built in part on an abandoned interurban streetcar right-of-way, was an early example. The three-lane highway with a passing lane in the middle prevailed before the war, with Ohio, Pennsylvania and New York leading in total mileage and New Jersey, Massachusetts and New York in percentage of mileage.

When George Washington traveled to Mount Vernon, he did so at the rate of Abraham traveling to Ur of the Chaldees. When Roy Chapin drove his Oldsmobile from Detroit to New York in seven-and-a-half days in 1901, he made slightly better time than the stage coaches on the route as the nineteenth century opened. The pony express would have scoffed at the time it took the first motorists to cross the continent. And yet by 1901 the speed of autos had so increased that Connecticut had to establish a speed-limit law, the first in America, twelve miles an hour on the open road and eight in cities and towns. Forty years later, the year of Pearl Harbor, the era of the railroad as a passenger carrier was headed to its close, the peak of travel by bus was approximately reached and nearly half the communities of the United States depended entirely on highways for individual and commercial access to the nation and the world. A transportation revolution every bit as significant as the revolution railroad travel had effected had come to pass, and the revolution simply continued and expanded when the war was over.

Our problem is not to amplify but to limit the theme. The revolution in the American vacation was no less fundamental, no less nearly total, than the revolution in travel itself. By 1940 travel was subject to individual control and the travel had become the central fact of vacation and not some destination. Furthermore, a basic fact about travel was becoming clear. It is natural to measure travel in miles, but it is equally logical to measure it in hours. If a driver can average fifty miles in an hour on the highway instead of his erstwhile twenty-five, at least in theory he can go twice as far in the same time as before. This in turn means that the radius of a vacation trip taken in the last two weeks of July is about twice what it once was, and in effect this means that if one starts anywhere in the midwest, both coasts are within range and if one starts on either coast certainly half the country falls within the arc that radius describes. From the Gulf Coast, Canada is not an impossibly distant prospect; from the prairie provinces, one can aspire to Texas and even to the Mexican border towns.

It is time to give some thought to Canada. There is no properly developed concept of the American vacation, one might even dare to say no rational concept, that does not find room in it for Canada, and of course the principle works in reverse. Today Quebec and Ontario plates are as common on Cape Cod and the Connecticut coast in the last two weeks of July as Massachusetts and Connecticut plates are on the streets of Montreal and Quebec. Indeed, as a Cape Codder the writer has come to recognize as one harbinger of summer the first Quebec plate seen on a Cape Cod road. What is more, he is now beginning to question the harbinger. The Canadians have discovered that winter golf is a one-day drive from Montreal. It is a shrinking world, whether one measures it by supersonic flights or six-inch putts. Let us move up to Canada.

In 1898 the Canadian customs officials faced up to an identity crisis. John Moody had reached the border and whatever he had reached it in had to pay duty if it was to enter Canada. It was fashioned like a buggy and had the wheels of a buggy. On the other hand, it was self-propelled by some contrivance stored beneath the seat. The customs officials, with that zeal for the fiscal well-being of their people so typical of them as a group, so admirable as a matter of principle, so worthy of imitation by other branches of the government and so little imitated, declared that it was a carriage and had to pay thirty-five percent duty. John Moody contended that its primary characteristic, self-propulsion, removed it from the carriage category. He contended, and the customs officials perforce agreed, that there was no provision for such a self-propelled vehicle as his in the tariff schedule and that therefore it had to be categorized by way of analogy. His brilliant thesis, to which the customs officials gave admiring if grudging assent, was that he was driving a locomotive and so should pay only twenty-five percent duty. He got in on that basis and drove his locomotive to Toronto. His one-cylinder Winton was the first automobile in Toronto and his saga, like the entire history of the roads of Canada which is a composite saga of often imposing proportions, may be found in Edwin C. Guillet's admirably written and splendidly illustrated *The Story of Canadian Roads* (University of Toronto Press, 1967).

There would be more, many more, automobiles in Canada before the passage of many years. Canada has two magnificent transcontinental railroads, but it has never had nor has it needed the elaborate cross-hatching of railroad systems characteristic of the United States and Europe. Immense as

Canada is, thickly settled Canada is a narrow band never far north of the border and *thickly settled* is itself a relative term justifiable as a rule only at wide intervals. Individualized transportation is natural in a country like Canada, and it is natural too that great areas do not need even the cross-hatching of roads characteristic of the thickly settled region and so can be served by airplane. There is no part of the United States of which this can be said except Alaska, where Canadian conditions prevail. Subject therefore to the limitations that a relatively small population imposes where land areas are immense, Canada buckled down to work as soon as the auto had proved itself and produced a good road system. The proportions of the task should not be underestimated by readers south of the border. Americans are accustomed to use Texas as a standard of immensity. Quebec is more than twice as large as Texas, Ontario and British Columbia very much larger, Alberta, Manitoba and Saskatchewan about the same size. Only the Maritimes are provinces comparable in size to the typical American states.

The first modern highways for automobiles in Quebec were built about where one would expect them to be built, from Montreal to the New York border and from Montreal to Quebec. The former was macadamized in 1912-1913 and christened the Boulevard Edouard VII. It joined at Rouses Point the American road which makes its way down the Richelieu and Hudson Valleys to New York City, making a comfortable and convenient route to Gotham and also making the long, circuitous, thoroughly desirable route to Boston already mentioned. The road to Quebec was finished as a hard surfaced highway in 1918. It hugged the river, passed through a number of quaint, fascinating, inexpeditious villages, took a long time to drive but gave you plenty to see. Highway 9, which is part of the Trans-Canada Highway, now crosses to the south bank of the St. Lawrence at Montreal, cuts a swath through mainly drab and dreary countryside, but brings you quickly and easily to the bridge below Quebec where you cross, make your choice from a cluster of motels or drive purposefully down the Grand Allee to the Chateau Frontenac with its bevy of satellite hostelries. It is a quick, smooth, thoroughly modern highway, but the other values belong to the old roads that hug the two shores of the St. Lawrence.

Ontario matched Quebec in the speed with which it reacted to John Moody's locomotive and its successors. As a matter of fact, John Moody would have been able to drive on a macadamized road from Napanee to Kingston in 1838, or to drive twelve miles out of Toronto on Yonge Street. The automobile did not create the hard-surfaced road. The ancient Romans had it, and so in our modest pre-auto way did we Americans and Canadians. The automobile made the hard-surfaced road essential and universal, after the railroad had made it almost obsolete. By 1915 Ontario had a concrete road between Toronto and Hamilton, and in 1939 it had in the Queen Elizabeth Way, which extends from Toronto to Fort Erie opposite Buffalo with a spur to Niagara Falls en route, the first superhighway in North America. The only roads to match it were the German autobahns. The Pennsylvania Turnpike, the first superhighway in the United States, was not started until 1940.

The good roads movement in the Maritimes and the prairie provinces gained headway that was rapid when one considers their population and size. Canada's smaller insular province, Prince Edward Island, presented a specialized and rather interesting situation where roads were concerned. The automobile maketh a bloody entrance into islands. Nantucket fought it tooth and nail, it was barred from Mt. Desert chiefly by its owners, Bermuda still bans it for visitors and Mackinac has an unblemished record of defense. But these are small islands, whereas Prince Edward Island is the size of Delaware. The automobile invaded Prince Edward Island in 1907, and was driven out in 1909. *Driven* is employed in the military, not the automotive, sense. The ban was partially lifted in 1914 when certain roads of the province were opened to autos three days a week.

In 1919 Prince Edward Island joined the automotive age. Assuming that this is meritorious (the point admits of being contested), credit should be given the province for two automotive firsts actually achieved long before the automobile itself came into being. In 1877 the province created a

Department of Public Works with road-building one of its responsibilities, and the same year it abolished statute labor. Statute labor was the happy practice, long in vogue on both sides of the border, of letting the local farmers work off their taxes by putting in a few days on the roads. These days were happy days, leisurely in nature, given to long and ruminative pauses in the toil, lending themselves to the gregarious pleasures among which should be accounted the jug, but not lending themselves to the construction of good highways. Prince Edward Island saw the light before any other province and before most American states. By 1923 the province had an 850-mile road system built by men who knew how to build roads, and in 1930 it began to cover their distinctive pink surfaces with smooth if somber macadam.

We have spoken of the drive from Boston to what have for many decades been two prime vacation objectives for Bostonians, the cities of Montreal and Quebec, and of the drive between them. There was, and still is, the other drive from Boston to Canada, the drive to the Maritimes. In recent years that drive has been modified by ferry service between Portland and Bar Harbor, Maine, and Yarmouth, Nova Scotia, and for many years there has been a modification of value to those with destinations in the southern half of Nova Scotia, the ferry from St. John, New Brunswick, to Digby. Since modes of travel between cities in no way affect the location of cities, it follows that the imperative of train travel which geography imposes on New Brunswick and Cape Breton Island, not to mention Prince Edward Island and Newfoundland, bars with equal effectiveness the palliation of travel by intermediate ferry to those whose fundamental conveyance is the family car. Boston to Sydney is just as much a land voyage as Boston to Chicago and always will be. But Boston to Sydney has not always been the long and comfortable swoop northeastward on an interstate highway to Houlton, Maine, a brief link between the nations over to Woodstock, New Brunswick, and then a comparably comfortable swoop southeastward on the Trans-Canada Highway. In the old days the swoops were there all right, but not the comfort.

To some extent Maine has a penchant for the sort of tidal river so common in the south, noble streams when the tide is in, less noble when it is out, but at all times apparently about as wide as they are long. There had to be a bridge across them, tides doing what they do to tidal rivers, but there certainly did not have to be bridges across real rivers like the Kennebec and the Penobscot. One crossed the Kennebec by ferry, a craft which always managed to time its crossings so as to allow the eastbound traveler ample opportunity to test the scenic and cultural attractions of Bath, Maine, and the westbound traveler to do the same in Woolwich, where they are even more sparse. On the other hand, one detoured northward to Bangor, the point at which the Penobscot was reduced to manageable proportions for those who built bridges in a day when bridges were not to bankrupt taxpayers by their costs nor travelers by their tolls.

From Bangor there were two ways to go. The conventional, appropriately sanctioned and moderately peopled way was U.S. 1 down the coast. One recalls how the Maine coast undulates—never more so than in far eastern Maine—and what hamlets there were clustered at the heads of bays and inlets. Route 1 made them all, using more than ample mileage in the process. There was another way, one for those abundantly blessed with the spirit of Cartier and Champlain. It is now Route 9 and except for some paving not always of the highest standard it is about what it was a half century ago, a ride of endless curves, rises and dips through a region almost as unpeopled today as it was just before the ancestors of the Indians made their way across Bering Strait, a road that offers to the wayfarer the services and accommodations one associates with the Gobi desert. On the other hand, it was and is very much shorter.

Beyond Calais (pronounced *callous*) lies Canada, and at this point we may leave our wayfarer of memory, confident that New Brunswick and Nova Scotia matched and even surpassed any problems of auto mechanics or logistics that Maine could contrive. But to many who drove the long and arduous miles to New Brunswick, Prince Edward Island or Nova Scotia there was to vacation the added surge of warmth that goes with coming home. Even to the rest of us Bostonians, to whom the ancestral hearth was more apt to be in Ireland or Italy than in the Maritimes, there was to the drive Down East something that no other drive had. At the risk of raising hackles in Chambers of Commerce, we had the feeling that Maine and the Maritimes existed simply and solely as what Maine on its license plates proclaims itself to be, Vacationland. They offered the new sort of vacation at its best, and there was about it something faintly suggestive of the Indian on the trail. The roads to New York and Washington should be good, but the roads Down East did not have to be, although there were no complaints when they were finally paved. One was philosophic about the traffic through Connecticut and New Jersey, or at least one was after the ordeal was passed, but one did not have to be philosophic about the traffic Down East. One expected none and ran into none. There was a comfortably shabby aspect to hotels Down East, except for the thoroughly spruced up railroad hotels in Halifax, but they made up in their homey quality for what they lacked in the attributes that were making Statler a household word. Furthermore one was free to range the countryside secure in the knowledge that although the roads left much to be desired and anything they did not leave to be desired the hotels did, distances were never long and half the fun of vacation lay in making nonessential the essentials of life. In those days when the vacation by automobile was in its lusty infancy, all roads led north from Boston in vacation time and no road was better than the long, dusty, unpaved one that wound in and out around the coast of Maine and finally reached that part of Canada which to so many Bostonians is not only Down East but also Down Home.

9. From running water to color TV

 A man once built three or four crude cabins. He did so on a hunch that refined itself into a prophecy, developed into an omen and at last was recognized and hailed as an inspiration. No one knows his name nor where to raise the tablet of enduring bronze that would mark the site of those three or four crude cabins, if three or four they were. Like the ultimate beginnings of many great achievements that create watersheds in the pattern of human life, the beginnings of the motel are lost to knowledge. It is a pity, for that man began a chain of events that revolutionized the entire hotel industry in the United States and Canada, and is casting ever longer shadows over the most eminent hostelries of western Europe.

There is a sense in which the motel is something new in the hotel industry, and a sense in which it is a return to something very old. In the Middle Ages the roads into the cities had their inns on the outskirts, just as American cities have their motels today. Geoffrey Chaucer's pilgrims started to Canterbury in 1387 from the Tabard Inn in Southwark, one of the string of inns lining the southern approach to London Bridge and serving the traveler who came from south and east of London and from the continent beyond. Today it would be the Holiday Inn and would have a swimming pool. What was true of London was true of every great city of Europe; motel row is at least as old as the Middle Ages, and doubtless older. It was the logical complement to travel by coach, carriage or horseback, just as the motel is the logical complement to travel by private car and bus. The really surprising thing is that it took so long for the logic to be recognized.

The modern city hotel is the creation of the nineteenth century and the railroad. Once travel was by rail and from one city center to another, the intown hotel became inevitable and the attributes that attend it: large size, many rooms, rooms as compact as possible, facilities for large-scale meetings, extensive dining and wining facilities. Close to the railroad station was a good location in one sense, a bad one in another. It caught the traveler who put convenience at the top of the list, lost the one who inclined to cleanliness and quiet. Electrification of the railroads has solved that problem in much of Europe, and in a European city or town one may count with almost certainty on the presence of a good hotel within bag-carrying distance of the station. It might even be argued that the city as we have known it is the creation of the railroad, and as the American railroad has dwindled and almost disappeared as a passenger carrier, the city has accepted the automotive age and has been diffused into the suburbs. The dwindling of the city hotels and the burgeoning of the suburban motels is a constituent part of the process. We shall leave to the sociologists the problem of fitting this rather angular fact into their demographic calculations as only obliquely pertinent to the history of the American vacation.

The man built his three or four crude cabins on the hunch that a man and his wife would pay a dollar each to spend the night in one and therefore not have to seek out the city hotel, or its usually nondescript country cousin, and pay a substantially stiffer rate. He furnished his cabins with stuff from the attic, from the bedroom his son abandoned when he married, from his late uncle's belongings that his aunt had left in the barn when she sold the farm and with a few odds and ends he picked up at the Good Will. The beds were brass, grooved and streaked with the years, or white chipped enamel; the chair (the husband could sit on the bed) was sagged pre-Grand Rapids dining room; the pitcher that stood in the bowl was refilled with water after the departure of each guest and the towel on the nail replaced from time to time; and the sanitary facilities we pass over in reverential quiet. No one expected the Waldorf Astoria for a dollar a night.

It worked. One has a feeling that it worked for a variety of reasons, a tangled variety not easy to sort out. Economy was an obvious reason, but economy itself is not a simple motivation. To one person economy is the fact of saving, to another the thrill of saving, to a third a personal triumph over the powers of aggrandizement, to a fourth the vindication of one's personal intellectual superiority as evidenced by success in getting the best bargain possible. There is nothing surprising in the fact that persons open-handed in most things are often surprising tightwads in little things. When the psychiatrists finish with the Oedipus complex they might try their hands at the Thrifty Scot complex.

Undoubtedly one reason was the thrill of the untested. It would have been simple indeed to drive into nearby Ozone City, take a room at the Mansion House, have the filet mignon with baked potatoes and string beans and after dinner see *Beau Geste* at the Alhambra Theater. You would know in advance just what you would get and what you would pay for it. But a night in the cabin would be an adventure and pot luck at the eating place down the road that the farmer said wasn't half bad would be another adventure, and if it was a mild night and you could sit out after supper, the summer sky on a cloudless night in the velvet darkness of the country can be a show to rival *Beau Geste*. Adventure was a part of the reason.

One feels that beyond this there was another feeling less simple perhaps to put into words, but not impossibly the reason that was dominant. One lived in the equivalent of Ozone City, with a comfort substantially greater than the Mansion House afforded. Ozone City and the Mansion House offered nothing by way of basic change. The thrill of economizing can be felt when one chooses and often when one does not choose, and never more easily, not to say perforce, than after a vacation. The thrill of dinner at a place down the road that isn't half bad can easily be exaggerated. But there was a feeling to spending a night in a tourist cabin with the most rudimentary of furniture, with a summer breeze that came in through the cracks in the walls about as easily as through the windows, a feeling that one was momentarily lifted from everything customary and familiar and left in a situation uncluttered by the commonplaces of everyday and stripped to the barest essentials of shelter and rest, and this feeling in some mysterious fashion was itself the reward.

About the best one can say is that for the moment one felt himself an Indian, an Indian on the trail, a child of nature momentarily close to nature and happy in the fact of reunion. The thrill of the tourist cabin by the roadside was to the state of travel what the thrill of the camp in Maine or Minnesota was to the state of rest. Bare, stark simplicity and a momentary surcease of civilization bred a happy illusion of their own, and between the husband in his shirtsleeves and the wife in what passed in the 1920s for leisure dress outside their cabin in the summer night, and John Muir on some sweeping escarpment in the Sierras without another human within fifty miles—but the glory of the mountains all about him and the majesty of nature lambent on him—there was a kinship. "It feels great to get away," was the ordinary way of putting it. The man who built the three or four crude cabins was indeed right in his hunch that people wanted to get away in that psychological sense. The instinct to play Indian is an ineradicable instinct and one of the happiest there is to satisfy.

Then simple and inevitable improvements began to appear in the tourist cabin. The other farmer down the road saw how his neighbor was turning the sweep of grass between his house and the road into a money-making device, and he determined to improve on the example. He installed plumbing of an elementary sort into the cabins he built and charged a dollar and a quarter a night. A man in the next township with a sharp and steady eye for a profit sensed that there was in this new business something suggestive of a future, and he built with the thought of the chill even of the summer nights in these parts and thought as well of the possibility of both anticipating the summer and prolonging it. He put a heating device in the cabins he built and charged a dollar and a half.

One recalls with emotion the heating device and the plumbing. The former was a dubious entity at the best, frequently constructed and usually operated on some principle understood imperfectly even by the fey contriver of makeshift machinery who designed it and the blacksmith who brought it into being. Asphyxiation was added to collision as a travel menace, and the prudent left it severely alone. The cold of an early autumn night is preferable to the cold of the grave, even under blankets from which years of use had extracted all but the suggestion of warmth.

The plumbing was another matter, inviting and justifying hilarity. In theory there was some device for providing hot water, but the theory remained untested. There was a jerkiness to the flow of water at any temperature, a moment of hesitation followed by a watery eruption and then a semi-steadying down to a thin and waving stream. What the faucets did in a minor way the shower did on the grand scale, alternating moments of quiescence with explosive bursts.

Emery's Black and White Cabins, Bar Harbor, Maine.

New York Public Library

Ablutions completed, one stepped gingerly from the upended, cast-iron coffin called the shower onto a piece of heavy paper called the shower mat which was decorated in yellow and purple with the image of some fish still unknown to sober ichthyology. Then one discovered that it was not heavy paper at all, but blotting paper with an enthusiasm for absorption and an amazing capacity for shredding, curling and nestling between toes. One dried in a towel of gossamer cloth capable of instantaneous and total saturation, and proceeded to distribute uniformly over one's body the wet from the shower. Finally one's clothing absorbed the water and one emerged from the ordeal invigorated, cheerful, vastly contented with life, bubbling with the happiness of having gotten away. Indeed the instinct to play Indian is an ineradicable one.

But there is another instinct equally ineradicable. The Indian's state is an unstable one, and it endures only so long. One's first encounter with a chilly night in a tourist cabin had all the thrills of novelty, but the second night had all the vibrations of discomfort. The next time the Indian instinct took possession and one took to the road in the new Chevrolet which had replaced the old Model T and had a self starter and a heater of sorts, one stopped at that newer sort of tourist cabin someone had christened a tourist court. The cabins were joined together by a single roof, with a space for the auto between the cabins. The discovery had been made that it was a little less expensive to build tourist cabins with a single roof, and that it was possible to have a single heating plant that actually heated the rooms safely and heated water as well. It cost the traveler a shade more, but it was more comfortable and safer. Without being aware of it, the Indian had taken the first tentative step toward becoming an aristocrat and the motel had been born. It was still an adjunct to the farmhouse in back and was considered nothing more than a supplementary source of income for the farmer's wife who swept out the rooms and made the beds. But the farmer and his wife were surprised after Labor Day when they added up the proceeds and saw how important a part of their livelihood this new venture was providing.

Thus the motel was born, but the modern motor hotel has an important collateral elderly relative in addition to its obvious ancestor, the traditional hotel. In its background is the tourist home. The tourist home was like a motor hotel in the obvious fact that it was a house, and the less obvious fact that it often served breakfast. The resemblance ends there, but the true basis for relationship is something different. There were travelers too elderly perhaps, too staid, too conventional, too fond of comfort, too uncertain of a night on the windswept plain between the farmhouse and the road, too possessed of whatever might have been the quality or composite of qualities that made them want to spend a night in a house and not a cabin, to accept the cabin as a substitute for the conventional hotel. On the other hand, they were quite ready to accept a tourist home with its economical price structure and its convenient parking. The tourist home habituated them to the fact that they did not have to drive into the heart of Ozone City and seek out the Mansion House, but could spend the night comfortably in a tourist home on the city outskirts and dine reasonably well at the place up the street which the lady in the tourist home said was really quite nice.

The heyday of the tourist home was the 1930s, and about it there always seemed to the writer to be something a little sad. It had to be located on a main thoroughfare and it had to be large enough to accommodate paying guests in addition to housing the owners. In other words, it was by its nature not the sort of house that was ever supposed to be commercial property and ordinarily the people who lived in it were not people who had expected to become innkeepers to provide an economic buttress for their sagging fortunes. It seems in retrospect that it was always a lady, in both senses of the word, who answered the bell when you stopped at a tourist home. If you got to know her, you discovered that she was a widow or that her husband had been incapacitated by a stroke or had had a heart attack, or perhaps you never did discover why she had to take in paying guests and sensed that it was in no way your business. Often during the Depression when the tourist home was so common—one does

not speak of institutions as having flourished in the 1930s—
her unemployed husband carried your bags to the room and
chatted with you for a bit, and you were aware that the man
who built or bought such a house had not always been a
bellhop. You were always aware in a tourist home that you
were in another person's home, a welcomed and indeed
eagerly sought intruder but an intruder just the same. Some
tourist homes became informal inns and some of them still
survive, and there of course that feeling of intrusion is not
present nor should it be. It was usually present in the tourist
homes of the 1930s, and their disappearance in such large
measure from the American scene should cause no nostalgia.
Yet memories remain.

There was the elderly Boston couple who lived on the river
side of Beacon Street. It is impossible to explain to one who
is not a Bostonian what it once meant to live on the river side
of Beacon Street, and it is unnecessary to explain it to one
who is. The Depression hit them with titanic force, but the
mightiest ocean hurricane can hit Gibraltar and it is not
disaster. They were elderly, their means of livelihood had
dried and withered away, they were too old for the jobs that
did not exist anyway and so were the cook and maid, so the
four of them turned the house on the river side of Beacon
Street into a restaurant and served dinner in the beautifully
appointed library that overlooked the river and the Harvard
Bridge and the Harvard crew. The menu was limited but the
cooking superb, the tables somewhat extemporized but the
silverware sterling, and the cloths and napkins were Ireland's and Belgium's best. One night there were two
desserts, snow pudding and pumpkin pie. The writer, with
the thought in mind of his mother's snow pudding that was a
cloud of ethereal ambrosia resting in a creamy pool of nectar
and aware that only here might it be equaled, asked for snow
pudding. Milady regarded him with a quizzical expression.
"We have pumpkin pie, you know." "I know. I think though,
I'd rather have the snow pudding." She left and returned
with the pumpkin pie. "I brought the pumpkin pie," she said.
"Snow pudding is no dessert for a man." There was discipline
in that house on the river side of Beacon Street, and one

respected it. It was a great happiness when one day the discreet little sign announcing the existence of an ordinary within disappeared and one knew that dividends had been resumed. One wonders if there is still that kind of courage on the river side of Beacon Street.

Back to the motel. Before World War II a subtle shift in emphasis came and the linked group of tourist units which had provided extra income for the farmer and his wife became their primary means of support. The 1920s had seen a mighty surge of hotel building in the United States and Canada, and the 1930s had seen a mighty downfall. It is estimated that four out of five American hotels either passed through bankruptcy or through the sort of drastic fiscal reorganization that amounted to the same thing. But at the same time it was discovered that a husband and wife could operate a motel of up to fifteen rooms and pay off their capital investment in five years or a little more. A rough and ready economics was being hammered out for the infant industry. The operator had to charge a dollar a night for every thousand dollars of capital investment he had made in his motel. Thus a room that cost six thousand dollars to build could be rented for six dollars a night and provide a handsome return. The rule of thumb still works fairly well today at a dollar and a half a night, but construction costs have soared far above six thousand dollars a room. The room that cost twelve thousand dollars to build must be rented for eighteen dollars a night to keep the fiscal ship afloat, but now we are talking in Holiday Inn–Ramada Inn–Howard Johnson figures and are far ahead of our story.

The pa and ma motel of fifteen rooms made money in years in which the Waldorf Astoria in New York and the Stevens in Chicago rolled up statuesque deficits. Discoveries were made in the construction of such. The carport proved unnecessary, just as it has proved unnecessary to the construction of the modest single house. Its elimination simplified the construction of the motel, which became essentially a row house structure with each "house" a motel unit. Better plumbing and better heating systems became possible, and some of the hallmarks of the primeval motel began to disappear. The upended coffin type of shower came to be replaced by the stall shower, and it was discovered that bathtubs with showers could be installed in motel rooms and pay for themselves in higher room rates. The blotting paper bathmat with its yellow and purple fish was replaced by the terry cloth bathmat, which might even bear the house crest if the motel was elegant enough. Towels became thicker, more absorbent and more numerous. The motel room came to have two comfortable chairs, an achievement that seems to have been beyond the power of all but a handful of American hotels. Even the wafer of soap which has been the traditional American hotel gesture toward cleanliness just as truly as the Gideon Bible has been the gesture toward godliness grew in thickness and surface area.

For years the typical motel was a rowhouse structure of up to fifteen or twenty rooms, with a parking space for a car before each and two chairs with plastic webbing on a shaded concrete porch in front of the window. One was still directed to the restaurant down the road, but now that there were three or four motels on the highway and several guest houses, the increase in business had made that restaurant decidedly more worthwhile as an investment and had upgraded both the quality and the variety of its cuisine. Indeed, what with its parking space, the cocktail lounge that was installed as soon as the national drought was repealed by the requisite number of states and the discovery that good meals can be served at highway restaurants and that there was nothing sacrosanct to the tradition of the disreputable roadhouse, the place down the road became the best place to eat in town and drew a good deal of local patronage away from the Mansion House dining room, a drab and humdrum place at the best with its undeviating half a broiled chicken, roast sirloin of beef and veal cutlet with meat sauce.

There was more than a touch of the small town to the ma and pa motel. You drove to your parking stall and took a surreptitious look at the license plates to left and right: Ohio, North Carolina, Pennsylvania (two) and a genuine novelty, Alberta. As you took your bags from the trunk, North

Carolina emerged from his room and called to your attention the goodness of the day. You agreed that it was indeed a good day. Two Pennsylvania juveniles came up and read your plate: Massachusetts. "Massachusetts. Is that Boston?" "No. It's Cape Cod." That stopped them for a moment. "Cod. That's a fish." You agreed that cod is indeed a fish, and a big one. They found it amusing that a state should be named for a fish. You let it go at that; etymology is not for all ages.

Meanwhile your wife had struck up a conversation with Ohio. Your wife's cousin lived in Youngstown and Ohio came from Cincinnati, but did not know your wife's cousin. She did have some thoughts, though, on the problem of washing, drying and ironing clothes in a motel room, an issue of no small consequence in pre-drip dry days, and your wife found her a very intelligent and interesting woman. You recognized some of your neighbors in the restaurant, and having dined in at least semi-contiguity you had a subject to start the conversational ball rolling when chairs were pulled together on the concrete porch in the evening. It was really Alberta and his wife who were the featured speakers in the colloquium. Their tale of wheat and its attributes, its perils and disasters as well as its triumphant wonders was a fascination, and they capped the fascination with their account of how the stout of heart could now drive to the Canadian Rockies and at places into if not quite through them. It was, of course, the old small city lobby moved outdoors, and there never was a better place to pass a sociable evening than the lobby of a small city hotel until the motel added fresh air and a total freedom from receptacles for cigar ashes that were last cleaned during the administration of Rutherford B. Hayes. The ma and pa motel has been superseded but not eliminated, and a good one is still a wonderful place to stop.

The impulse to build larger motels and thereby make more money was a potent one. Like many impulses of its sort, what was thought bedrock in it was really a quagmire. It is not obvious that a motel of thirty rooms will make more money than a motel of fifteen. It isn't even true. Ma and pa could take care of the fifteen room motel, but once they got

An early tourist camp.

over fifteen rooms they had to hire help. By and large a motel should have at least fifty rooms to make it profitable to hire help, and it should have more than fifty if it is to be profitable to an absentee owner. Once the motel reaches the three figure mark in rooms, increase in size can be translated into profit at a very high rate. One more clerk and four more maids can take care of a 150-room motel as compared to one of one hundred rooms, and their wages at the most do not amount to more than fifteen percent of gross sales. But like all other trees, the motel tree does not grow to the sky. No motel should be too large for the business of its area, and the problem of providing a parking space for every motel room becomes a major one as the motel grows above 150 rooms. An auto needs about 350 square feet of parking space, including its share of the driveway. Land costs can be indeed a major fact in the construction cost per room of a motel, and the rule of thumb that one must charge a dollar and a half a night for each thousand dollars of construction costs per room is a valid one.

No generalization is true in all particulars, and this principle applies quite as well to generalizations about motels as it does to all man's deeds and ways. In general, however, the ma and pa motel was successful and by 1951, according to *American Motel Magazine*, there were 43,356 motels in operation. A motel built in 1951 probably had somewhat more than fifteen rooms, was located outside the city but not too far from the city line, had neither a restaurant nor a swimming pool, had a public telephone in the office or in a booth on the grounds, was rather apt to have a radio in each room and just possibly might have a pay television set, and was exclusively a place at which traveling men and tourists spent the night. There was no provision for daytime activities and certainly no provisions for meetings. By ten in the morning the motel was somnolent, not to awaken until well into the afternoon. In between ma made up the rooms and pa cut the grass, replaced the washer on the faucet in number eighteen, helped ma bundle the laundry and then, if their luck was good which it very seldom was, they turned to the wisdom of the Latins and had a brief siesta. On Sunday, with luck, they got to church, and once in a blue moon visited friends. The moon had to be almost navy blue to make that possible. A motel was a good investment, but it was as bad as a dairy farm for keeping you tied down.

In 1952 a motel was built that was to change the basic foundation of the motel business and make it come of age as age is understood in late twentieth century America. A native of Osceola, Arkansas, named Kemmons Wilson, who had started his career at the age of fourteen as delivery boy for a drug store and at the age of seventeen had operated in the lobby of a movie house a popcorn business at least as prosperous as the movie house itself, had parlayed that through five pinball machines and a venerable airplane in which he gave dollar rides into a construction business which had attained a liquidating value of $250,000 when he went into the service in World War II.

Donald E. Lundberg tells the story of Kemmons Wilson and Holiday Inn in his *The Hotel and Restaurant Business* (Chicago, 1971). Mr. Wilson, his wife and children had returned from a vacation trip marred by the worst accommodations in his memory, made none the better by exorbitant rates. He knew that he could do very much better than that, and he surmised that he would prosper mightily if he did. He built a motel in Memphis and called it Holiday Inn. It was so successful that within a year he built three more Holiday Inns in Memphis. The motel business was waiting to be brought to age. These four Holiday Inns represented a leap forward into the virgin territory which lay between the conventional city hotel and the small scale motel. They furnished the easily accessible free parking and the self-service freedom from tipping of the latter, but they offered as well full restaurant service, a free television set in each room, a swimming pool, easily available ice cubes, a telephone in each room, facilities for meetings and what is most important of all, a reliable and satisfactory uniformity of accommodations. As his idea caught on and Holiday Inns began to sprout around the country, he worked out a referral system which permitted a guest at one Holiday Inn to make without cost a reservation at another. Obviously the more motels in the chain, the more potential guests, and the more valuable the motel itself to the person who held the franchise. It would be futile to say how many Holiday Inns there now are, since any figure stated becomes obsolete within a week. Let us merely say that the number is now making appreciable inroads into the four figure area.

In 1954, two years after the first Holiday Inn was built, something new appeared beneath the orange roof of Howard Johnson. The best known restaurateur in American history had become an innkeeper. Kemmons Wilson started in popcorn, Howard Johnson in ice-cream cones. There is a stretch of Boston Harbor coastline south of the city known as Wollaston Beach. It has never been compared with Daytona Beach for the quality of its sand, nor with Nice and Cannes for elegance, but it is close to Boston and in the well populated city of Quincy, and it is a good place in which to cool off when the summer sun is hot and the time for travel limited. Howard Johnson decided that Wollaston Beach would offer a solid market for ice-cream cones and he might thereby bolster the somewhat shaky economy of the drug store he had inherited from his father. His secret of success was ridiculously simple: he made his ice cream of the best possible ingredients and he experimented with every nuance of flavor he could conceive. The result was top quality and endless variety; his twenty-eight flavors is as grave an understatement as Minnesota's ten thousand lakes, if experiments and discarded models are included. The writer well remembers the lines that stood outside the booths Howard Johnson erected at Wollaston Beach in the 1920s, waiting with only token gestures at self-control for the ice-cream cones his staff of high schoolers vended.

The first Howard Johnson roadside restaurant was built on Morrissey Boulevard in Dorchester, a suburban sub-division of Boston, a site in those days passed by almost every commuter who drove from his home south of the city in the morning and back again in the evening. Breakfast at Howard Johnson's on the way up and ice cream for the family on the way back became part of many a driver's ritual. For that matter, it still is at the same restaurant. The fundamental Howard Johnson formula was present from the start: the general American quick order menu of ice cream, hot dogs and hamburgers for the hurried, and table service featuring fried clams and steak and presented to the leisurely in a pleasantly decorated dining room. Just as Kemmons Wilson created a reliable and satisfactory uniformity of accommodations at his Holiday Inns, so Howard Johnson created a reliable and satisfactory uniformity of food at his roadside restaurants, and then transferred the principle to his motor lodges. Presumably today Howard Johnson motor lodges rank next in number to Holiday Inns, but census estimates are too hazardous in an industry still bubbling with development as the motel industry is. Obviously Holiday Inn and the Howard Johnson motor lodge begat the rest: Ramada Inns with their attractive colonial design and in general their superior dining rooms; TraveLodges with their gaily tiled sides, their scaled down operation with the customary absence of a restaurant and the frequent absence of a swimming pool, but the usual, highly welcome presence of a lower room rate than their competitors'; and the magnifico of roadside motor hotels, the Marriott, a full-scale city hotel in every respect except its usual country setting, its ample parking, and the subtle way in which it flavors city hotel amenities with a whiff of resort hotel atmosphere. Then there are the motel associations like Quality Courts, Great Western Motels, Superior Motels and the others which are uniform only in the excellent quality of their accommodations and which offer all sorts of variety within the limits of variety possible in motels.

There is something in all this with which to conjure. Once upon a time a farmer built three or four crude cabins on the stretch of grass between his house and the road and rented them for a dollar a night per occupant. Those occupants were Indians, in our specialized sense of the word. In the genes of those crude cabins was the Marriott Motor Hotel, an abiding place for the traveling aristocrat if ever there was one. It is somehow an ineradicable characteristic of the American people that anything successful is glorified and transmogrified out of all imaginable resemblance to its simple, primal self. The cabin proved successful, and grew into the Holiday Inn. But the cabin was not unique in this respect. Consider the game of golf.

Golf was once a simple game in all respects except successful performance. It required a large tract of land, swathes of which had to be mowed for fairways and patches manicured to serve as greens. Players required a small sack of clubs and a fair number of balls. They could carry the clubs and lose the balls without assistance. Then the caddy appeared, to carry the clubs and find the balls. The game grew in popularity. Then the scientists got to work on the clubs and balls, introducing niceties of construction into both which were hypothetically translated into lower scores but were certainly translated into higher prices. Then the clothing people got into the business. They had their heyday in the 1920s, when a sort of golfing uniform was created consisting of baggy pants called plus fours and an expensive variant of the cap worn by all small boys of the period. The growing popularity of the game, with a hearty assist from the Depression and with the presence on the golf course of a proletariat to whom a few years before golf had been an unfailing source of merriment in the hands of such entertainers as Gallagher and Sheehan, put an end to the golfer's uniform. But as the proletariat took over, the private club became more and more a necessity for those who wished the entire ritual in its unsullied form: the locker room, the place to entertain the visiting buyer, the Scotch on the rocks in the locker room, the dining room, the social center for the family and therefore the swimming pool for the younger fry. All of this commanded, and still commands, its price. Then the machine age invaded the sylvan scene, and the notable discovery was made that by riding in an electric auto the avid golfer could play twice as many holes and eliminate entirely the exercise for the sake of which he claimed to have taken up the game. Both goals were speedily achieved by the forward looking.

Next the entrepreneur took over and provided sternly disciplined golfing services for the enthusiast on vacation and away from home. At his home club the golfer retained at least a measure of independence, and was forced into the golf cart only by peer pressure. Some golfers were sufficiently independent, or independently wealthy, to ignore peer pressure and continue to plod around the course, pulling their club carts behind them. But on vacation independence was perforce sacrificed. At the fabulous seaside course in which one had automatic membership for the duration of his stay at the fabulous Florida or Caribbean resort, not only was the golf cart obligatory but frequently the front caddy, a human retriever whose function it was to flush the errant golf ball from its covert in the rough. The result is the current Florida foursome, which resembles nothing so much as a highly organized and expensively equipped safari combing the bush for big game in the African veldt, with the beaters out in front, the heavy equipment behind them, and the hunters armed with a dazzling range of armament from Abercrombie and Fitch and fortified by the illusion that if good old Sam Snead can do it at his age, so can they. The other result is a cost of $30 per player per round.

Back to the motel. In the approximate quarter of a century since Kemmons Wilson had his unsatisfactory vacation trip and invented Holiday Inn in self-defense, that pattern of uniformity dear to the American heart, and the pledge of reliability it connotes, developed on American highways from coast to coast. It is probably safe to say that it is impossible today to get more than one hundred miles from a Holiday Inn anywhere in contiguous America, possibly safe to say the same of Howard Johnson Motor Lodges, and it seems reasonable to assert that if one is determined to see America with every morning a fresh start from a Ramada Inn, a Quality Court, or a Best Western, it can be arranged with a modicum of planning. It is probably safe to add that one may lunch every day as he wends his leisurely way through the forty-eight states on a McDonald's hamburger or on Kentucky Fried Chicken, granted a list of their locations. We have seen how the motels started, but the pattern of uniformity on the highway and the related pledge of reliability started in 1925, when A&W Root Beer granted a franchise to J. Willard Marriott and from it emerged Hot

Shoppes. The franchise concept made possible the uniformity, which people often dislike, and the reliability which they
desire. Who first brought inconsistency into the human heart
is lost to knowledge, but it happened long before the time of
Kemmons Wilson and Howard Johnson, McDonald's hamburgers, Kentucky Fried Chicken and Hot Shoppes.

The one fundamental, profound and richly significant
change that has taken place in the American vacation since
its inception in the days when people sought health at
Saratoga and salvation at Chautauqua is that it has changed
from a pattern of rest to one of motion, from the vacation at
the resort hotel to the vacation on the road. As Americans
travel today on the interstate highways which an incalcula-
bly large number of their tax dollars have provided, a radius
of approximately half the width of the country can be drawn
from any home in America. The outer perimeter it describes
marks off the area one can reach by car in the last two weeks
of July.

Americans really know their country today in a way the
railroad generation never knew it, and those who maintain
that this tends to intersectional understanding and tolerance
might do well to add to the sophisticated intellectual
arguments they employ the prosaic contribution made by the
fact that Howard Johnson has the same basic menu in
Massachusetts and Oregon, and that Holiday Inn bedrooms
in Minnesota look like those in Mississippi. There are those to
whom uniformity is abhorrent, and they detest these facts,
and there are those to whom uniformity is reassuring and
desirable and they cherish them. The success of Howard
Johnson and Holiday Inn suggests that there are more who
crave uniformity than detest it, and the uniformity of the
ragged jeans and straggly beards of our official non-confor-
mists suggests that they also are conformists, but in their
own way.

The truth is that the real John Muirs and the genuine
Henry David Thoreaus are never numerous, and never can
be identified by their personal appearance. The Kemmons
Wilsons and Howard Johnsons who can parlay popcorn and
ice cream into national enterprises, not to mention Harland

Sanders who, starting at the age of sixty-five with a Social Security income (yes, Virginia, there is a Kentucky Colonel) and a fried chicken recipe brought Kentucky Fried Chicken into being and made it the largest chicken franchiser in America, are even less so. No human power is quite so rare as true originality and true originality means, not the ability to cut a path through the woods and up the mountain that no one has cut before, but the ability to cut a path to a place no one else knew existed.

None of this really matters to the family with the last two weeks in July at their disposal and the family car packed and ready to go. Man succumbs to uniformity but nature never does, and no area of comparable size in the world except Europe rivals the United States in natural variety. The highways of America offer access to God's plenty, and the enterprise of America takes ample care of the vacationist's physical wants while his range of spiritual desires, sparked by that divine discontent that is present with some intensity in every human being, finds a measure of satisfaction. It may be beside a lake in Maine or a cascade in Oregon, in the swaying grasslands or the Rocky Mountains, for the Westerner when he first sees the Atlantic and in imagination the heritage from which he sprang, for the Easterner when he first sees the Pacific and has his own wild surmise on his private peak in Darien. He may spend the night physically at Holiday Inn or Howard Johnson's, but spend it spiritually in a place that has no name, because it is of the essence of travel that it is not arrival and that there is always that other place farther on of which one dreams.

10. *Winter vacations*

 One of the supreme discoveries in the history of the American vacation has been that a vacation can be taken in January as well as in July, and better still in both. Like many American discoveries of the sort, it followed by several centuries the establishment of a European commonplace. Britons discovered centuries ago the winter delights of Italy and Portugal, and once the short and grim autumnal prelude to the British winter had set in, many of the affluent were safely afloat on their way to Lisbon, and the more venturesome on the long sea road to Naples, the gateway beyond which lay Florence and Pisa, warmth and sunshine. The Riviera and what it connoted came in due course. Later the Germans made the same discovery, and those fiscally able to flee the horrors of the Scandinavian winter were also prompt to do so. After the political and economic historians have finished explaining the closeness of the ties that historically have existed between Britain on the one hand and Italy and Portugal on the other, the travel agents can explain the rest. Britain has many charms and merits, but it has no Florida. Italy and Portugal for centuries have filled the role of Florida for Britain.

The familiar pattern of acceptance was as necessary for that novelty, the winter vacation, as it had been for the summer vacation. First, the grandparents of the jet set had to discover the American South, a discovery that was delayed by their preoccupation with the European South. Furthermore, they had to pin down their discovery so that at least the suggestion of permanence might be present in it. There was something in the ancestors of the jet set who ruled the land in the 1880s reminiscent of the sand pipers who trot the beaches of Cape Cod for a few short days in August. For some days they are there, and then one day they are gone and no one outside ornithology knows whence their travels nor whither. Their coming is as reliable as the passage of the moon and the stars, and their visitation as short as, in Hamlet's opinion, woman's love. So with the jet set of the 1880s. The accolade they gave a place was impressive, but exceedingly transient.

They gave their accolade to Aiken, South Carolina, on April 1, 1882, when the first polo match was played there. Its setting was worthy of its importance: lavish lunches in the sylvan dells, gay cross-country rides by vacationing lords and ladies on steeds appropriately caparisoned, a dress drill by the Palmetto Rifles but, as the Charleston *News and Courier* rightly noted, ". . . all this paled into insignificance before the brilliant and successful introduction of James Gordon Bennett's popular national game, polo. It caused a great sensation, and completely revolutionized the city as far as amusements are concerned." Aiken has never completely outgrown the revolution. It has had its textile mills and its refining plants for clay, but it has had as well its fox hunts, its drag hunts, and whatever else field sports may offer.

Annually there have dawned its fleeting days of glory as it has become a playground for lords and ladies, and then they have gone their way to other and more northern bowers of bliss, to Southampton, Newport, Bar Harbor and the rest. Once more the ordinary folk of Aiken have been free to walk their quiet streets, and at least look into the parks where southern pines mingle with oaks and magnolias, and nature herself is an aristocrat. No one came to Aiken in search of salvation, and polo has never enjoyed the favor of competent physicians as a health-promoting activity. Consequently winter did not enjoy the twofold benediction of vacation in the North, health and salvation, but vacation reached the South just the same and it was brought there, to the extent that it was an imported product, as it was brought to Saratoga Springs and places of its sort by the lords and ladies who emerged from the pristine state of American big business late in the nineteenth century. There is another

Aiken, South Carolina became the polo capital of the 1880s jet-setters.

point of importance to be noted. Vacation in Aiken was associated with a particular sport, polo. Far more than the summer vacation, the winter vacation has tended to be sports-oriented, although the sport is usually less rarefied than polo. It may be golf, it may be skiing. The locale may be Florida, it may be Vermont.

There is another point not merely to be noted but to be stressed. There is a certain tendency in the North to think that Northerners discovered the South. This is not true. Northerners no more discovered Palm Beach than Southerners discovered Cape May. Yet there is something innocent in this illusion that the North discovers the South or the South the North, or for that matter that the East discovers the West or the West the East. Vacation should be grounded firmly on illusion and enjoyed in a state of euphoria. As a matter of sober fact Southerners have always known that the South is studded with places where those blessed with good judgment are able to spend very pleasantly what days of leisure the winter offers and, not considering themselves kings, not pay a king's ransom for the privilege. Except where a handful of original thinkers is concerned, all such words as these are wasted on the frosty air of the North when the last two weeks in January roll around. The average Northerner knows the South by name, and its name is Florida.

We said at the outset that certain strips of sun-kissed coast and certain ridges with snow-capped peaks have been endowed by the vacation with an economic and even political importance they would never have enjoyed were it not for the sun and the snow. We cited Florida and Switzerland as examples and we might quite reasonably add to Switzerland such states as Vermont and Colorado. There is no doubt that the northern two-thirds of Florida was economically viable without the aid of winter visitors, with full allowance for all they have added to its well-being, but the same can be claimed with less certainty for the southern third. It had one pearl beyond price, the most reliable winter warmth in continental United States, but a realistic appraisal of its other pearls would trace most of them to the five and dime store. The point may be established by a comparison of Florida then and now, even with our *now* stopping many years before the actual present.

Below Indian River, a name immortalized in India ink on grapefruit, is a once isolated section formerly known as Lake Worth. It may be defined for our present purposes as the area from Palm Beach to Miami. In 1876 thirteen persons lived there, all related. They had bought the land for a shade over a dollar an acre. One interested in Floridian antiquities can poke around the grounds of the Royal Poinciana, for it stands upon their acreage. It was a simple life at Lake Worth, and no place in the South was better suited to the vacationing Indian with a taste for the remote and primitive, the simple and unsullied. The best place to encamp was east of Lake Worth, in a section known locally as Palm Beach. That became its official name in 1886, when a post office was opened there. Until it was opened, if there was mail it got as far as Titusville by established methods and then anyone who happened to be going down to Lake Worth brought it down. Hardly anyone lived in the barrens between Lake Worth and the Miami River, although adventurous souls penetrated them. It is part of the record that one pioneer failed in his efforts to get a friend to accompany him to Biscayne Bay when the latter countered with the charge that there was no such place.

The railroad, however, was making its inexorable way south, and in 1888 it threw out a long tentacle from Titusville. This spur was eight miles long, had stations at Jupiter, Mars, Venus and Juno, and was known unofficially as the Celestial Railroad. Jupiter and Juno, at least, are still on the map and Juno became a place of such consequence that for ten years it was the seat of Dade County. It was even possible by the 1890s to make one's way south from the railhead at Juno to Biscayne Bay by a stage coach known as the hack line. The trip took two days and if there were more than five passengers, the democratic procedure was that all should take turns walking. A seventh son of a seventh son might ponder as he trudged the rutted, sandy path that he was walking by Palm Beach, Delray Beach, Boca Raton,

Deerfield Beach, Pompano Beach, Fort Lauderdale, Hollywood and Miami. From these modest beginnings made possible by vacationing Indians from the North came the glories of the lordly present. No tribute could be more magnificent to Fahrenheit and his works.

It took more than vacationing Indians enamored of the simple and unsullied to make Miami even a mirage. It took Henry Morrison Flagler, a founding father of Standard Oil and its organizational genius; it took the railroad that he built from Jacksonville to Key West; it took the luxury hotels with which he punctuated and glorified the East Coast; and it took the promotional and organizational inspiration that he brought to play upon the problem of making the Florida East Coast the Riviera of America. Flagler's instinct was for the south, for the Biscayne Bay area below Palm Beach, for the lowlands with horizon at eye level beyond, for the step across the water to Key Largo, and the other stepping stones across the waters to Key West. Thus far and no farther a railroad could go, but Flagler was determined that it would go the distance. On January 22, 1912, the first train of the Florida East Coast Railroad reached Key West and Flagler's work was done. A year later he died.

The proto-history of Miami is fairly typical of the entire East Coast, except that its remoteness and difficulty of access give it a more rugged character. Some prescient writer for the St. Augustine *News* stated as early as 1843 that the one suitable place for a town between Indian River and Cape Florida was the Miami River. Seven years later the legislature put a thousand dollars on the line, for the building of "a proper wagon road" down to Miami from Indian River. But vastly more important than prophecy or appropriation was the arrival in 1871 of Mrs. Julia D. Tuttle of Cleveland, Ohio. She came down first for the health of her father and then of her husband. When the latter died, she bought from the Biscayne Bay Company 640 acres on the north bank of the river and then told a fellow Ohioan and subsequent business associate of Flagler's, J. E. Ingraham, about her vision of a city of Miami. He was intrigued enough to come to investigate, proceeded to get lost in the depths of Seminole territory, and to be rescued by an Indian friendly with Mrs. Tuttle. Ingraham was sufficiently impressed despite his woes to transfer allegiance from Henry B. Plant, who had investments across the great diagonal from Jacksonville to Tampa, to Flagler whose faith was pinned on the East Coast. He brought with him the allegiance of Mrs. Tuttle, who offered Flagler half her holdings if he would bring his railroad to Miami. Flagler, who was in a period of rest and recuperation, felt that a steamer from Lake Worth would serve Miami nicely. It is a strange fact about Flagler that he was gloriously right about the East Coast as a whole and strangely wrong about particulars. He saw little by way of future for Miami, but had a vision of Key West as a major port and metropolis. An unprecedented freeze in December, 1894, perversely thawed Flagler's determination and made him dream once more of his railroad across the seas and his private Dark Tower, Key West. He got to work on the railroad extension, had new towns plotted along its route of which Fort Lauderdale was to be the most important, and on April 15, 1896, the first train pulled into Miami. With Flagler's aid the incipient city was still called Miami. Many wished to call it Flagler.

In the proto-history of Miami one meets Mrs. Tuttle and then Flagler. In time other names became important. There is the name of George E. Merrick, whose brain child is Coral Gables. Merrick was an aesthete as well as a financier, and Coral Gables was to be an artistic triumph as well as a financial one. Every house had to pass the scrutiny of a board of architects; zoning of business and manufacturing was to be rigid; spacious plazas, golf courses, polo fields, a yacht basin and other nuances of the good life were to await those who lodged at its elegant hotel or moved onward and upward to membership in its superlative country club. Rex Beach wrote the brochure, for $25,000. William Jennings Bryan preached its gospel at the Coral Gables Venetian Pool for forty minutes a day and $50,000. Buses scoured the bush from New York to San Francisco, with "Coral Gables" emblazoned on their sides and an invitation to prospective buyers both warm and loud. Lesser Coral Gables were launched at Hollywood and Boca Raton. The former countered the eloquence of William Jennings Bryan with the massive prowess of General George W. Goethals, builder of the Panama Canal, as supervisor of its harbor installations and its major land construction. Addison Mizner, architect of Palm Beach, conceived of Boca Raton and in six months brought it into being, with its golf course, its two hundred homes, and at least the foundation of its Ritz Carlton Hotel. At that he really missed the boat because, to switch metaphors, the tide was already running out.

The Florida boom peaked in 1925. The state with an incredible future dealt mainly in futures. An investor, as the self-deluded speculators called themselves, invested in binders. A binder was an option on a piece of property for which a quarter of the purchase price was due in thirty days. The game was to sell the binder to someone else at a profit before the thirty days were up, the profit averaging as high as fifteen percent. The purchaser's game was to do the same to someone else, and so ad infinitum. But it was not to be ad infinitum. It was to be until September, 1926.

The boom peaked in 1925, but that very year the clouds began to gather. First a lady's hair curler caught fire, the fire spread, the Palm Beach Breakers went up in flame and the Palm Beach Hotel with it. Then a discarded Danish training ship, the Prince Valdemar, purchased to be a gambling haven somewhere in the deep blue yonder, went aground in Miami harbor sealing it completely with some eighty ships locked inside and an indefinite number outside. By ironic coincidence this was the time that the Florida East Coast Railroad and its competitor the Seaboard Airline which, with wisdom or folly, also had entered Miami had to suspend operations while tracks that would hold cars properly were installed. Then there was a nautical encore, as another vessel grounded in precisely the wrong place. Next the National Better Business Bureau launched a probe of ethics in the Miami land trade and found none. In February, 1926, the New York stock market slumped badly enough to put investors in a defensive position on the north-bound trains.

Miami Beach in its heyday as a resort, 1923. Nautical mishaps, temporary suspension of rail service, two devastating hurricanes and the stock market crash combined to diminish Miami's booming growth as a vacation mecca during the closing half of the decade.

Then came the September hurricane, one of the worst in American history, and two years later another hurricane. Three years later the stock market crashed. *Sic transit gloria Miami.*

And yet the truth about Miami was not the shattered shards of the dreams of those who dreamed of being millionaires and awoke to bankruptcy. As things worked out, the truth was the dreams themselves and more than the dreams. After the cold, gray morning that ushered in that drab and dreary decade, the thirties, and the war years when Miami was a training area deluxe for the services, the dreams began to become reality. Modern Miami began to appear in the years directly after the war, grew to full and flamboyant maturity in the 1950s, and in the decades that have followed Miami has become Greater Miami, and flamboyance greater flamboyance. One may select from the gamut of emotions one's preferred emotional reaction to Miami, but one thing is certain: reality has surpassed the dream, whether one deem it dream or nightmare. The maddest castle built by Ludwig the Mad of Bavaria dwindles by comparison with Fontainebleau and Eden Roc, Surfside Tower, Manhattan Towers and Seacoast Towers. Lords and ladies of the court of the Sun King never lived as the lords and ladies of the Flamingo lived, and their children at the sequels to that noble hostelry, the Algiers, the Carillon, the Saxony, the Sherry Frontenac and the rest. Lords and ladies gaily girt attending a tilt at arms in Tours wore fustian by comparison with our latter-day lords and ladies wildly waving tip sheets at Hialeah. There is something mad about Miami, and probably that madness is its best excuse for being.

One might very reasonably ask why this last and most remote finger of land pointing down to the swamplands and the tepid waters beyond, where one finds nature tolerable for a third of the year at the best and relies on nature improved and methodized by air conditioning the rest of the time, has become the greatest single concentration of vacation facilities in the world. The best one can say by way of explanation is that the human race has a way of spinning faster and faster until centrifugal force produces a central vortex into which those who chance the perils of the spin are inevitably drawn. The primal reason that Miami exists we have already mentioned: winter warmth is more reliable there than anywhere else in continental United States. The habitual pattern of development is just as visible in southern Florida as it is in other vacation lands. Some pioneer, with that rarest of human attributes, true originality of vision, first finds the place and has a vision of its possibilities. First there is a Mrs. Tuttle, who intrigues a J. E. Ingraham, who convinces a Henry M. Flagler. But before there could be a Miami as Miami came to be, there had to be a Palm Beach. The native American aristocrat, whose 'scutcheon is emblazoned with dollar bills, must first make the area fashionable. Then one of two things happens: either the aristocrat of the first generation is driven out and the aristocrat of the second generation replaces him, or the older aristocrat holds the fort and the newer aristocrat builds another fort nearby. In southern Florida Palm Beach held out, and therefore Miami came to be. Miami has this in common with the winter wonderland of southern Arizona: they are the two continental resort areas that developed as a result of the solving of the ancient problem of time, rate, and distance by the airplane. The fact that Miami is on the last and most remote finger of land in eastern America makes no difference, since you can fly there while your relatives, who drove you to Kennedy or O'Hare, are trying to get home through city traffic. And so Miami grows, and last year's fabulous hotel is eclipsed by this year's fabulous hotel, which rests uneasily in the shadow of next year's fabulous hotel as it rises where once there were sand, shells whole and half broken, bits of weathered ···ormy wood and tall, green, undulant grasses that waved their plumes and held south Florida together.

We have not finished with the winter vacation when we have traced the sage old birds to their winter lairs deep in the South. There remain the snow buffs and the extraordinary vacation phenomenon that has developed out of the basically simple act of sliding downhill on two sticks. Between St. Petersburg, Florida, and Stowe, Vermont, there is a mileage gap of about 1,500 miles and an age gap of about fifty years. At the age of seventy a person goes out of winter if he can; he goes more deeply into it at the age of twenty. If crossed shuffleboard cues might grace the municipal crest of St. Petersburg, skis rampant could do the same for Stowe.

One recalls the plain beginnings of the sport which today as from the very start mainly flourishes north of Boston and west of Denver. Skis were sold at the sporting goods counter of the local department stores and at the specialized stores that dealt in a range of products connected with athletics. The bedrock business of such places was in baseball and football equipment, with the rapid flowering of interest in golf a titillating if somewhat speculative matter. What were then known as bathing suits, logically enough since they were essentially two piece suits even if an ingenious one piece affair into which an athletic young man could wriggle was becoming a vogue, also loomed large in the economics of the sporting goods trade. But this new interest in skis, like the somewhat earlier and rapidly developing interest in hockey, was viewed with substantial interest by entrepreneurs in athletic wherewithal. Winter was a drab and dreary season in the sporting goods trade, once Christmas and the investments in baseball and football futurities it elicited were over. The ski and the hockey stick might do something to take up the economic slack. Hockey was obviously a Canadian import and a very important one in Boston, which is a semi-Canadian city anyway. The ski was vaguely associated with Scandinavia, as the yodel is with Switzerland. However, if there was a dollar in it, Boston merchants would sell it. No doubt the same was true in Denver.

There are hills enough in Massachusetts, but snow in Massachusetts is as unreliable as it is undesirable. In Vermont and New Hampshire, on the other hand, snow is as trustworthy as the Green and White Mountains themselves, and over in New York the Adirondacks become Christmas card mountains before November is far advanced. The sport at first was simplicity itself. The participants strapped their skis to the top of the car and drove to the nearest hill in New Hampshire or Vermont that was covered with snow and belonged to a farmer good natured enough to let young people slide down it. One walked to the top, slid to the bottom, walked to the top, slid to the bottom, repeating the cycle until the thigh muscles made it transparently clear that they had had it. Then the participants strapped their skis to the top of the car and drove back to Boston. It was simple downhill work of the straightforward sort, unembellished with fancy maneuvers identified by French names. This included *après ski*.

The first stage on the inexorable march toward complexity and expense which every popular American activity takes was the ski train. The writer imagines that the ski train was the brain child of someone employed by the Boston & Maine Railroad; at the very least, the B&M was ready and waiting for the idea as it dawned. The thesis held by aficionados of the sport that the railroad waxed wealthy on them was totally without foundation. It is part of the unhappy record that the B&M never waxed wealthy on anything, and its management and stockholders alike would have been substantially better off if it never snowed at all in northern New England. But snow it does, in highly measurable quantities, and tracks must be plowed anyway. If snow could be turned into money, the B&M was ready and willing. The snow train made the deficit of winter operations at least melt along the edges.

North Conway, New Hampshire, was as highly desirable a destination for the snow train as ever was developed. New Hampshire is a state that improves with penetration from south to north. It has a southern tier of counties which, when full allowance is made for the charms of the Monadnock region, has been chiefly valuable as a residence for poultry destined for the broiler and for people fleeing Massachusetts taxes. Above this tier comes a lake country of substantial beauty, and with good winter sports potential. Next nature quiets down for a while, but toward the pole star lie North Conway and the White Mountains. Science showed its potential for the skier at an early date in North Conway. Slopes were manicured, hoisting devices installed, inns refurbished, motels erected, dining and wining facilities provided and a town which had long enjoyed a steady but not titanic popularity as a summer resort discovered that the big money is in what had been deemed the dead season. Today it is soberly reported that the Cranmore Mountain skimobile can carry 1,000 passengers an hour, and that the North Conway hospital is a world center for the setting of broken arms, collar bones, and legs is universally accepted by the medical profession.

There is an important distinction between the ski season and the Florida season. The ski season is basically for those who work, the Florida season for those who are retired or at least in a position to take off a week or two. The ski season is far more a weekend proposition, a happy respite to the week's routine, although there are skiers fortunate enough to get a winter vacation and to spend it on the slopes. There may have been blessed individuals fifty years ago who were enthusiastic about skiing and in a position to indulge themselves in its delights for a week or two in the winter, but there were certainly not enough of them to create a pattern nor to make twitch the sensitive antennae of the resort operators and the travel agencies. But the future never shows the cards it holds in its hand. Today the winter vacation is an esteemed bonus for the college students whose academic year has been as systematically shortened as the tuition bills their parents pay have been increased. With the long stretches now in which the groves of Academe are out of cultivation the winter vacation for youth is a fact, and very frequently a fact of economic advantage to such a state as Vermont.

Vermont illustrates quite as well as Florida what organized vacation operating as a big business can do for a resort area. If one considers Vermont in the state of nature, before any Green Mountain was furrowed for the convenience of skiers, it is hard to escape the conclusion that Vermont used to be a five month proposition. Spring is a rugged season in the Green Mountains, marked by chilling blasts, drenching rains, miry roads, and snowstorms after the thought of snow had dwindled into the unhappy remembrance of things past. But all things end, even Vermont springs, and by June the state is once more habitable for out of staters. What follows is five of the most glorious months enjoyed by any state: June that is green as only Ireland is green, July and August with pleasant warmth by day and a coolness that descends upon the land at sunset, September with wine in the air and gathering russet in the woods, and then October that riots with reds and yellows until one night a voice speaks from the northland and the show is done. Until the ski took over, as it showed incipient signs of doing in the 1920s, wavered in the depressed 1930s, but gathered unabated momentum after the war and has kept gathering it ever since, one can picture a prankster hanging at the Massachusetts and New York borders on October 15 a sign that read, "Closed for the Season." Today one can picture his son who runs the local inn hanging up in serious reality the sign that reads, "Open for the Season." The change has been a steady one, as the Vermont weekend of skiing came to include an anticipatory Friday and a postprandial Monday, and then was lengthened by the fortunate so that the two weekends met harmoniously on Wednesday, and the ski vacation was born. It is not a phenomenon that can be dated with accuracy. The writer's guess is that the potential for growth was already there in the late 1920s for one prescient enough to see it, but that the momentum really started after the war.

The result is that today Vermont comes closer to being a four seasons vacation land, without the use of airline or resort blandishments, than any other state except its rival Colorado. As the foliage dies away, the first flakes flutter down. Skis are waxed, ski tows tested, motels quietly shift gear into winter rates and restaurants stock up on all that makes for *après ski*. The morning is soon upon us that dawns dull and gray, but Mount Mansfield has been buried during the night and the season is opened. For five more months Vermont is open for business, with ski conditions improving and worsening periodically and each change of condition reported by TV, radio, and press in Boston as if the only way New England business could prosper was by sliding down hill. Then spring forces its chill and drippy way into Vermont and Bromley succumbs, then Sugarbush and Killington, and

WINTER VACATIONS · 171

finally Stowe falls and the year is over. What is left are April and May, grim and bleak, and then one morning it is June and a car with New York plates drives into the motel.

There was another form that the incipient winter vacation took half a century ago that must not pass unmentioned. We have paid our tribute to the vessels that sailed the seven seas from the port of Boston, but in particular sailed the portions of them that wash the coasts of Maine and the seaboard states to the south. We thought of them as passenger vessels and naturally were encouraged to think of them as such by their owners, but in large measure they were floating freight trains, especially those to the south. But there was one route that was sailed by the vessel for passengers and in all but the literal sense for nothing else. That was the two night and a day sail to Bermuda. One should note that it was a sail and not a cruise, a boat ride with a destination more important than the ride itself.

There are aspects of the world of vacation that turn upside down concepts based on geography or on national sovereignty. There are places in Switzerland that are really British. The Canary Islands are really German and Swedish. The Swiss own all of Switzerland, to be sure, and no one can counter the claim that the Canaries are Spanish by sovereignty, but where the local economies are concerned, the visitors set the pattern and once their numbers become legion the places which exist because of them exist for them. In similar fashion it is not quite true to say that for decades the beaches of New Hampshire and southern Maine have been Canadian, and specifically Montreal, beaches but it is not quite false either. In this sense it can be said that Bermuda is a Boston island.

Naturally this statement has to be made with the Pickwickian escape hatch open. Canadians have always gone to Bermuda in substantial numbers and now with British Airways making Bermuda a stop on one route to the South Seas more and more Britons are discovering its charms. Furthermore, Americans who did not come from Boston have been known to stroll on Front Street in Hamilton. But when all is said and done, Bermuda for generations has been a prime winter objective for Bostonians happy enough in their circumstances to have winter objectives.

Today Bermuda is a brief morning in the air from Boston. Fifty years ago it was not quite a cruise but it certainly was a voyage. There was the evening sail down the harbor, the first night afloat, the full day at sea, the second night afloat and in the morning one walked down the gangplank, crossed Front Street and entered the fine stores across the street from where the boat docked. There is only one Bermuda, and it used to be a land of an utterly different order from the known and familiar. It was a land of horse drawn carriages that kept to the left. It was a land where toast was dry and crisp and came to the table in racks. It was a land of tea, not coffee, and a land in the era of drought where liquor was legal. It was a land of flowers at a time of year when there should not be flowers, and a land of trees and bushes that were not familiar but suggested the tropics and weather far hotter than Bermuda knows. It was a land that was warm and friendly, beautiful, serene and beguiling, but above all a land that was foreign. Fifty years ago, when Europe was outside the fiscal range of most Bostonians and outside the vacation span of all but school teachers, Quebec in the summer and Bermuda in the winter gave many vacationing Bostonians their first insight into foreign lands and ways. The trip to Bermuda was one of the earliest forms the winter vacation took for Bostonians and other New Englanders, and it has never ceased to be one of the best.

Thus the last two in January had begun to unfold their possibilities a half century ago. The prime desideratum was warmth, but the secondary was its opposite; one turned to the warm sun, but also to the cold snow. The ski weekend was a reality, but it would be forcing time backward in its flight to claim that there was then anything resembling the ski vacation. On the other hand the Florida and Bermuda vacation did exist for natives of the Boston area. Clearly Miami was for the vacationing lord and his lady at their lordliest, and presumably Bermuda like Palm Beach was for the cultivated aristocrat who preferred his ease at a quiet, well bred watering spot.

It forces our metaphor too much if we attempt to equate the ski enthusiast with our metaphorical redskin. There is no reason to imagine that the real Indian ever regarded snow in any other light than does the city motorist today, except to the extent that it aided him in hunting, and if he wore snowshoes it was to expedite his progress and he neither expected nor got enjoyment from their use. If he ever slid down a hill on anything resembling skis, history is resolutely silent on the subject. Furthermore, there is nothing in the *après ski* conduct of the beautifully appointed Vermont ski resorts suggestive of the wigwam or the tepee. There are times to use metaphors and times to forget that they exist, and this time is of the latter sort. It was indeed one of the supreme discoveries in the history of the American vacation that a vacation can be taken in January as well as in July. The discovery was made well before the 1920s, but that was the decade in which it began to be developed, a word appropriate to southern Florida, and savoured, a word appropriate to Bermuda.

II. *L'envoi*

 L'envoi by definition is a concluding address to a prince or princess, lord or lady. It would seem that it might also be a concluding address to an Indian, brave or squaw. I have attempted to tell the early history of the American vacation, partly in the semi-sober terms appropriate to a history of its sort and partly by way of what the scholars, with their penchant for burying the obvious beneath the weight of words, call *exempla*. That is to say, to illustrate what the early history was like by ransacking the uncouth cells where memory lurks for illustrations drawn from vacation as it used to be when the starting point was Boston. You never can be sure about what you dredge up from those uncouth cells. Shreds and chunks of reminiscence have a way of combining inaccurately, and factual error is an occupational hazard for those who look, not in their hearts but in their memories, and write.

This really does not matter, since one can brazen it out in several ways. One can claim to be writing one's memory of what old time vacations were like, and there has always been a statute of limitations to protect the one who mingles pleasant fiction with half-remembered fact in the sacred name of nostalgia. One may also claim that he looks into his heart as well as into his memory and writes down the record of the latter as filtered through the former. As T. S. Eliot so wisely observed, the present is always changing the past, and the degree which nostalgia reaches in any generation reflects obliquely that generation's judgment of current life. We are living in a day when nostalgia is a vogue, as well it might be in the light of what the modern world has become. But that is not in itself a bad thing. If the present constantly changes the past, so the present constantly molds the future. Let nostalgia have its head sufficiently and we might move bravely and steadfastly backwards, and if it was better then than it is now, that is the right direction in which to move.

No one today intends to take the vacation of fifty years ago and yet it might be that in its early history and the *exempla* which illustrate it there are hints valuable for the vacation of today, and just barely possibly hints to a philosophy of life. What is more, there is very often present in the vacationing family one or more members who work steadily in the interests of the past. It has been profoundly said that there are two classes of travel, first class and with children. Nothing reduces the traveling lord and lady to the traveling brave and squaw quite so quickly as two or three little kids.

The instinct of the child is for the Indian's vacation, and it is an instinct that will not be silenced. The wise parents of little children do today what their parents did: they seek out a cottage or a camp where the beach shelves gently and the water is calm, they dress down to the thin line which prevailing propriety considers its outer bounds, they pare down the essentials to the barest few needed for rational survival, and they find that the more they live it down, the more they live it up. Chesterton once said that an inconvenience is merely an adventure incorrectly considered, and their vacation teems with inconveniences that become adventures. As the last two in July melt away, they find that they have been living simultaneously in their parental present and their childhood past, and they may bring back from the camp by the lake a greater awareness that time, place, and age are irrelevant to truth, and that one of the facets of ultimate truth reflects the radiance of the happy family, secure in the fortress that love, protection, and contentment have erected.

Time passes and the children grow, and as always the conviction rears its head that there is a link between travel and education. There is little of educational value to be gained by bringing the children to the Grand Canyon if they are still of an age to remember the Grand Canyon as the

Family shore picnic.

place where they had the hot dogs. On the other hand, it is no argument against going to the Grand Canyon that the children will remember it for the hot dogs. Vacation should be for fun and fun alone. Any extra dividends it pays in health and education are indeed extras and should be so considered.

This is not to deny that much of the fun of vacation comes from the thrill of discovery. The discoverer need not be stout Cortez on a peak in Darien. It is part of the endless charm of leisure hours wisely used that the thrill of discovery may come from the finding of a windflower too carelessly hidden by nature to escape discovery just as truly as it may come from one's first sighting of the Pietà. The cottage by the lake two hours drive from home grants peace of heart to the one who finds it there. For him the vision of the blue mosque in Istanbul is not necessary. We submit that the Pietà and the blue mosque are logically for youth. One of the great advantages the young now have in being able to see so quickly the great, entrancing, distant places of the world is that they have left for later years the small, endearing, nearby places. Perhaps it is not wise to leave the Taj Mahal for the golden years. Perhaps instead it is wise to leave for later years the small state park not far from home. Perhaps part of the serene wisdom is to recognize that life contracts as truly as it expands, and that the cottage by the beach that shelves down gently to where the calm water laps, the thought of which fires the mind of childhood, also casts a peaceful gleam upon the mind of age. As the years increase life's circumference contracts and the radius of travel grows shorter, and it shortens until the hour when suddenly it is infinite and the voyage into eternity begins. But for most of us there will be other Julys and freedom in the last two weeks of them. Perhaps our memories of how we used to spend those weeks may help the reader wait until it is again July, the bags are packed, the car is ready.